AMBIGUITY IS THE ANSWER

Ambiguity is the Answer

TIMELESS STRATEGIES FOR CREATING CHANGE

KYLE CRAWFORD

FALLOW PRESS

NEW YORK

Copyright © 2024 by Kyle Crawford
All rights reserved.

ISBN: 979-8-218-40621-9
Library of Congress Control Number: 2024906722

Fallow Press
228 Park Ave. S #193520
New York, NY 10003
www.fallowpress.com

For information on bulk purchase discounts or to request an
author speaking engagement, please visit fallowpress.com

Printed in Canada on recycled paper

It is brave to be involved,
To be not fearful to be unresolved.

— GWENDOLYN BROOKS

CONTENTS

Introduction	1
MAKE IT. PROTECT IT. PASS IT ON. *Ambiguity as Precursor*	5
TRUST IN THE LONG ARC *Ambiguity as Acceptance*	19
CONFLICT COMES *Ambiguity as Tension*	28
WHEN THE METRICS DON'T MATCH *Ambiguity as Split*	39
RETREAT AND RISE *Ambiguity as Options*	47
METABOLIZE MOMENTS *Ambiguity as Interpretation*	59
REMEMBER THE POWER OF SECRETS *Ambiguity as Protection*	69
LOVE YOUR LAYERS *Ambiguity as Completeness*	78
NOISE IN THE SILENCE *Ambiguity as Connection*	89

KEEP MOVING 100
Ambiguity as Advantage

HARNESS HIDDEN TRANSCRIPTS 112
Ambiguity as Accuracy

NEVER UNDERESTIMATE FLUIDITY 120
Ambiguity as Opening

THE APPEAL OF NOT KNOWING 131
Ambiguity as Attraction

INTRODUCE ALTERNATIVES 141
Ambiguity as Intrigue

A DISTINCTIVE CHARACTER 151
Ambiguity as Form

Conclusion 162

Notes 169

Acknowledgments 191

A Note on the Type 193

Invitation 195

AMBIGUITY IS THE ANSWER

INTRODUCTION

This book stems from the simple supposition that too many of our efforts to make an impact fail and our world would be better off if they didn't. And so this is a book about how to get things done. Not the tedious tasks that fill our days and have us chasing productivity tips so we can cram even more into 24 hours. But the big things. Work capable of nudging the world in a new direction. Projects worth dedicating our lives to. The kinds of successes that make a difference and leave a legacy.

The paradox is that for people who long to make a bigger impact many of us are painfully ineffective at doing so. This isn't usually due to the factors we're told matter. Many of us are comfortable generating new ideas, working incredibly hard, and surrounding ourselves with great people. We don't lack passion or brilliance. Rather, the difficulty sits beyond these, when we encounter the power dynamics invested in keeping things the way they are.

Navigating the competitive maze is always a harsher and more complex experience than expected. Though we are often told it will be otherwise, people are rarely waiting with open arms to embrace new approaches. Even those at the top of their fields must make their way through situations where they don't control the outcomes. The odds really *are* stacked against the success of what so many of us are trying to achieve. There is always someone with more power, connections, and money. *Always.* If our work is likely to pose a challenge to the status quo, then we need to be better prepared for pushback. And we need better strategies to guide us than the dominant storyline provides.

We do ourselves a disservice when we uphold faulty narratives that prevent more of us from succeeding in the face of opposition and obstacles. Without an understanding of what truly enables people to overcome even seemingly insurmountable challenges, I am worried that over time we will lose our ability to achieve the level of impact we desire. We will set ourselves up to fail again and again, simply because we didn't know how else to move.

The purpose of this book is to answer a timeless question: *How do we succeed in environments where the odds are stacked against us?*

INTRODUCTION

This is not a question that lacks answers. In fact, the issue is the opposite. The same approaches have been rattled off so many times they've become rote and restrictive. The path to success has collapsed into an insufficient storyline as though big ideas, hard work, and a strong team are all that's needed. We inherited this myth and too many of us have made the mistake of believing it. Because when the odds are against us, the dominant storyline is never enough. What's missing may tell us a lot about who benefits from the prevailing doctrine, as well as guide us to much more creative and effective paths.

I went searching for answers.

Who won when they shouldn't have? How did they actually pull it off? What's consistent across a wide range of competitive environments? What ends up making all the difference?

Over and over, I have found that *ambiguity is the answer.* It's like we were given a playbook with the most critical chapter ripped out. Across fields and throughout history, it is the production and embodiment of ambiguity that gives people an upper hand when it looks like they have none. In this book, ambiguity will emerge as the critical factor for success in social movements, sports, politics, art, business, and a host of other areas where people are trying to take themselves, their organizations, and their communities to new heights in the face of opposition.

Of course, we don't typically view ambiguity as an asset. We see it as the kind of variable that interrupts our plans, a

3

nuisance we're forced to deal with as a result of our complex and ever-changing world. Even the embrace of ambiguity that exists early on in new endeavors often comes with the recognition that, sooner or later, it's to be edited out and eliminated.

You'll notice that the prevailing perspective is rooted in the idea that we simply *respond* to ambiguity. This makes sense, as many of us are tasked with navigating environments rife with information that's contradictory and open to multiple possible interpretations. A large body of psychology research makes it clear just how poorly we respond to these types of ambiguous circumstances. When we add in even minor, unrelated stressors—deadlines, hunger, noise—we do even worse. We turn nuances into binaries, rush into decisions, and refuse to change our minds. No wonder we want ambiguity gone.

But focusing on the difficulty of response comes with an added consequence: *We're forgetting how much power there is in creating and embodying ambiguity.* As a result, we're at risk of losing much needed wisdom for succeeding in environments where the odds are against us.

Ambiguity Is the Answer is rooted in the discovery and fundamental belief that, in circumstances where we're outmatched, ambiguity can offer the protection and possibility we need to succeed anyways. Ambiguity is the answer we've been looking for. How and why we can use it to make the impact we desire is the focus of this book.

MAKE IT. PROTECT IT. PASS IT ON.

Ambiguity as Precursor

Our greatest responsibility is to be good ancestors.

— JONAS SALK

In the years before he went through a contentious and drawn out confirmation hearing, and before he distinguished himself during more than two decades on the Supreme Court, Thurgood Marshall had a story he liked to tell. It begins with a man walking down a sidewalk as a crowd runs by him in the street. Curious, this man gets the attention of someone in the back of the group who is struggling to keep up.

"What's going on?" he asks the person at the back of the crowd.

The straggler looks at him, annoyed at the question and the delay. "Don't you know I'm the leader of that crowd?" the straggler answers. "And if I don't run like hell they'll get away from me altogether?"

AMBIGUITY IS THE ANSWER

Before another question can be asked, the straggler takes off running, trying to catch up to the group they are supposedly leading.

Marshall's punchline is a simple one: The leader has *already* been passed. Whether they realize it or not, the shift they're trying so hard to prevent is already underway.

Marshall was considered one of those rare individuals who was just as comfortable talking with a stranger on the street as he was presenting a case in the Supreme Court. He was as intimately familiar with the U.S. Constitution as he was with injustice, having seen up close the devastation caused by white supremacy, and how states and communities green-lit mob violence. He knew how rights were trampled in schools, voting, the privacy of people's homes, and just about everywhere, in fact, one looked.

"His were the eyes that had seen, up close, men and women grasping for freedom," wrote Wil Haygood.

Marshall helped write the constitution for the newly independent nation of Kenya. A home he once slept in was blown up with dynamite so powerful it lifted the chimney out of the ground. He escaped with his life, just barely, more times and in more places than seems imaginable.

At a meeting in London, a prince once asked if Marshall cared to hear his opinion of lawyers. Grinning, Marshall replied, "Only if you care to hear my opinion of princes." After all, Marshall had dealt with the intimate condescension of politi-

MAKE IT. PROTECT IT. PASS IT ON.

cians like Bobby Kennedy, and was well-acquainted with the arrogance of the privileged.

This is all to say that Marshall, who was brilliant and full of experience, did not lack for stories to tell. *He had stories.* He had all kinds of them. So what was it about a leader failing to grasp a change was underway that was so intriguing to him? What clues does it give us for how he helped to bring about lasting change? And what might it tell us about the connection between diligence and ambiguity, in the face of resistance, that might inform our own work and our own lives?

As anyone who has led a team or launched a new initiative knows, larger visions only come to life if the little things are done right. Clarity and diligence are godsends. They operationalize the abstract and put us on the same page, rallying us toward a common goal.

This is why one of the big fears with ambiguity is that it will prevent us from getting things done. It can waste our time, cause frustration, and keep us from achieving our goals. But the utility of clarity shouldn't blind us to the benefits of ambiguity. The two are not always at odds. Rather than being caught in a zero-sum game, their relationship is more symbiotic. The key is to learn how to toggle between them effectively, to see how rigor and specificity in certain places can feed a useful ambiguity in others. In fact, the precursor to significant change is often a period of ambiguity brought about by impeccable work.

AMBIGUITY IS THE ANSWER

A case in point comes from the year 1905. In physics, it's remembered as *annus mirabilis*, or the *miracle year*. In that single span of the calendar, Albert Einstein published a series of papers that set a new foundation for modern science. At the time, Einstein was in his twenties and was disappointed in his achievements so far, having set his sights much higher than he'd been able to reach. No impressive companies tapped him for his talents. No fancy universities wanted to hire him. Instead, he was stuck working in a government building reading and reviewing patent applications.

Yet the bland position came with a benefit that even Einstein underestimated at the time: he was being paid to look at problems and solutions across a wide spectrum of areas. One day might find him dissecting the mechanics of a new invention. The next might force him to consider the issues at play when synchronizing time across space. Einstein paired this broad range of inquiry with his past knowledge in order to formulate some of the world's most powerful new insights, which he laid out in four watershed 1905 papers.

The first paper proposed the idea that light could move in packets as opposed to solely as waves. This idea went on to influence the concept of wave-particle duality used in quantum mechanics, and was cited in Einstein's receipt of the Nobel Prize.

The second paper helped lead to the acceptance within the scientific community of the existence of atoms.

In the third, Einstein proposed his theory of special rela-

MAKE IT. PROTECT IT. PASS IT ON.

tivity, where he argued that while the speed of light is fixed, as we get closer to traveling at the speed of light, space contracts and time dilates.

As if these were not impactful enough, in the fourth miracle year paper Einstein gave the world its most famous formula: $E = mc^2$.

Each paper was a landmark in itself. Collectively, they ushered in a new era. But *how much* they changed things was not immediately obvious. Like a specimen held up and considered, the implications of the 1905 papers took time to be understood. Before providing new clarity and setting the world in a new direction, they gave rise to a period of immense ambiguity, which prompted more questions than answers.

Where Einstein happened into looking at an array of issues, Thurgood Marshall sought it out. As the founder and head of the NAACP Legal Defense and Educational Fund, he oversaw some five hundred cases per year. People wrote to the organization for help on all manner of issues and the Fund helped everywhere it could. This gave Marshall tremendous visibility into the many varied forms of discrimination, and he used the unique vantage point to inform his legal strategy, intent on moving the nation closer to equality than it had ever come.

By casting a wide net and taking on so many cases, Marshall gave himself more options for unraveling segregation. He was rigorous in selecting which cases to push furthest, and he built a creative, outspoken team around him to craft their most promising constitutional arguments.

AMBIGUITY IS THE ANSWER

As one attorney who met Marshall said, "He had a peculiar and abnormal instinct about which substantive cases could come together. Like ocean waves."

Those who sought to uphold segregation might know *what* Marshall wanted to achieve but not *how* he would get there. They had no idea of the degree to which Marshall had dissected the body of law. When they looked at him, they saw an underfunded lawyer taking on too many difficult cases. While, in reality, Marshall was carefully introducing specific court cases and establishing new legal precedents. To do it, he had to protect the overarching strategy and make sure every little detail was right.

There is an old abolitionist saying that if you surround a scorpion with a ring of fire, as the flames move in closer and closer, the scorpion will eventually sting itself to death before it gets burned. The idea is that sometimes you have to start at the edges, raising the temperature and increasing the pressure.

For Marshall, segregation was the scorpion and each legal victory was a flame. He made no bones about his aim to eradicate the immoral practice of segregation and ensure the same constitutionally granted freedoms and protections were enjoyed by everyone. Marshall was unequivocal in his beliefs and backed them up with his actions.

Like Einstein's papers, each carefully crafted legal victory gave rise to new questions. *If this is a constitutionally protected right, then what else is? If these institutions can't discriminate, where else might it be illegal? Where can we light the next flame?*

MAKE IT. PROTECT IT. PASS IT ON.

Our successes often fall quickly into history, but for Marshall life was structured differently. His work was not a collection of discrete acts but a rich tapestry of strategic and mutually reinforcing threads with lasting impact. He was meticulous and outspoken without giving away the game. Marshall was solving problems as they arose *and* creating a legacy of cases to protect those in the future who would otherwise be harmed.

"He was trying to change the law so that precedence would be put into play," law expert Nicole Austin-Hillery said of Marshall. "It was a long-term game plan focused on changing the legal system of the future."

Don't be mistaken, though. Marshall may have been methodically lighting flames around the scorpion, but he was not one for delay. Urgency is never felt the same by those who are in power and those who are not. Marshall refused to succumb to the claim so often promised and so rarely realized that the best way to access rights that were already overdue was to *wait* even longer, to give it just a few more years or decades or centuries. He knew how the future was meant to look, and how much needed to be done to bring it about.

In a classic essay, Albert Camus explored this inherent tension of dealing with the world as it is while at the same time envisioning and enacting a new one. He wrote, "The artist constantly lives in such a state of ambiguity, incapable of negating the real and yet eternally bound to question it in its eternally unfinished aspects."

AMBIGUITY IS THE ANSWER

Though artists and attorneys may seem to be on opposite ends of a spectrum, Marshall operated similarly. There was no denying the reality of U.S. law—expansive, intrusive, disproportionately applied—and yet there was so much that clearly remained unrealized. It was, similarly, *eternally unfinished*. And, for Marshall, that call to make the law do what it was capable of doing for people's lives, even if it would remain a never-ending effort, was a worthy one.

Marshall devoted his life to a fight that began before him and would continue after him. He lived as what adrienne maree brown has referred to as a *future ancestor*. Carrying forth practices of emergence and adaptability, while always keeping an eye on a much further tomorrow, Marshall envisioned his work far outliving him and bettering the lives of those who never knew him personally but who, through the freedom of their own lives, would be connected to him forever.

He faced a dilemma each of us faces. At a time and in a world with no shortage of issues in need of being addressed, how do we choose between direct action and changing systems? How do we decide to split our time between the most immediately achievable good we can do, and the greatest impact we can make over the long term? This "delicate balance of turmoils," as a *Time* magazine profile on Marshall put it, can gnaw at each of us as we sift through our options for making the best use of ourselves.

There is no perfect balance for how to use our time and energy, but our decisions are made better by being rooted in a

MAKE IT. PROTECT IT. PASS IT ON.

context greater than ourselves. It is in the consideration of our ancestors that we gain our humility, and in the recognition of ourselves as future ancestors that we grasp our responsibility. We should aim to be people to whom others will be honored to claim lineage. In the moments that test us most, we must ask ourselves which move makes us a better ancestor? Which actions will tell future generations that they were present in our minds and bodies, that we carried them with us through everything and, in a way, they carried us through as well?

The cases Thurgood Marshall left behind for us read, as one attorney general put it, "like a map of crossroads on the journey to equality." Their names represent an almost short-hand of national turning points. Their dates offer a sobering meditation on all the harm done in the light of day. Though their importance may be clear today, originally they were each but one case in a stack of hundreds.

In *Sweatt v. Painter*, Marshall singed the first scorpion edges of school segregation. When the University of Texas School of Law refused to admit a young Black man named Herman Marion Sweatt due to race, Marshall appealed on the basis that there were no other law schools in the state. Texas quickly threw together a temporary law school for Black students, told Sweatt to go there, and dismissed his case. Unsatisfied by such a scheme, Marshall took the issue to the Supreme Court, which ruled that if public graduate and professional schools did not separately exist for white and Black students, then Black students must be admitted to previously all-white institutions.

13

It was a critical, if narrow, flame, as the Supreme Court ruling came with legal justifications Marshall would use in the coming years to tackle the issue more directly.

In *Smith v. Allwright*, Marshall successfully argued that it was unconstitutional for political parties to restrict participation in primary elections exclusively to white people, as they had been doing. The ruling overturned a unanimous court decision just nine years earlier that had enabled the injurious practice to continue.

Marshall took on the legally sanctioned, and often violently enforced, practice of segregation through housing covenants in *Shelley v. Kraemer*. These formal agreements required that homes could only be sold to white families, which enabled white Americans to extract essentially every bit of the generational wealth benefits from massive government programs like the New Deal and the G.I. Bill. At the same time, banks and real estate agencies worked in tandem to keep people of color, especially Black families, captive in neighborhoods where those same entities choked them off from access to capital and the ability to move to nicer homes.

To illustrate how wide-reaching this formalized segregation practice was on the part of white families, three of the nine Supreme Court justices had to recuse themselves from the case due to the fact that they owned homes with restrictive covenants in place.

"It shows how deep the case cuts when one-third of the

MAKE IT. PROTECT IT. PASS IT ON.

nation's highest court disqualifies itself," Marshall's legal mentor, Charles Houston, told reporters at the time.

Marshall garnered a unanimous decision from the Court that enforcing racist covenants violated the Equal Protection Clause of the Fourteenth Amendment.

Far from finished, in 1954, Marshall produced what is arguably the most noteworthy legal victory in U.S. history. In *Brown v. Board of Education*, the Supreme Court ruled unanimously that separate was not and never could be equal, finally overturning an 1896 case that had been wielded to justify harmful and exclusionary practices in all realms of American life. Focused directly on the issue of segregation, Marshall laid out in stark detail the wholly disparate conditions of schools Black and white children attended, making it clear the quality of schools was nowhere near "equal." Additionally, the Court ruled that even if the conditions were the same, forcibly segregating children on the basis of race was inherently unequal, violated the Equal Protection Clause of the Fourteenth Amendment, and had demonstrably deleterious effects on the outlooks and accomplishments of children. *Brown* opened the door to overturn segregation everywhere.

"I was so happy I was numb," remembered Marshall, when he reflected on hearing the ruling.

All told, before becoming a Supreme Court justice, Thurgood Marshall argued thirty-two cases before the Court as a lawyer and won an astounding twenty-nine of them. He argued another nineteen as solicitor general, winning fourteen. These victories did not occur in a vacuum, however. Marshall and his team were buoyed by the efforts of everyday people pushing for racial justice. As historian Howard Zinn has reminded us, "Behind every one of the national Government's moves toward racial equality, lies the sweat and pain of boycotts, picketing, beatings, sit-ins, and mass demonstrations."

Like Einstein's miracle year papers, to produce just *one* such landmark victory in Marshall's field would qualify as a remarkable career achievement. To produce all that he did is unparalleled. His diligence produced a broader ambiguity that served as a precursor to a fundamentally new future.

Marshall and Einstein had another, seemingly minor, characteristic in common as well. For all of the honors and recognition they received, both typically turned down requests to accept awards in person. Maybe they were concerned about appearances, not wanting it to look like the point of their work was to garner attention. Perhaps they were unmoved by the pomp and circumstance. Either way, they were both thoughtful about how they used their public presence.

Belying his usual approach, in 1946, Einstein accepted an invitation from Lincoln University, a small school located about an hour outside of Philadelphia that was the first historically Black college or university in the country to grant degrees to Black graduates. He spent part of the day going through his work on relativity for the students. Then he gave an address to the graduating class. Einstein had been appalled at how

MAKE IT. PROTECT IT. PASS IT ON.

the United States treated Black citizens, and saw a number of similarities with how Jews had been treated in his native Germany. In his speech, he decried segregation, calling it "an American tradition which is uncritically handed down from one generation to the next."

Genius though he was, on that day, there is much that Einstein would not have known. For instance, he would have had no way of knowing that the young son of the school's president who he spoke with that day would go on to participate in one of the most impactful civil rights organizing groups, the Student Nonviolent Coordinating Committee, as well as serve in government and as Chairman of the NAACP. Einstein would also have been unable to foresee that a Lincoln alumnus named Thurgood Marshall would do so much to prevent segregation from being handed down to another generation.

In 1978, after serving on the Supreme Court for eleven years, Marshall also made a rare commencement address. His was at the University of Virginia in Charlottesville. Marshall knew that the work of democracy is never ending, that the fight for equality always consists of advancing the cause, watching our successes be clawed back, and then having to push forward again and again.

Marshall told the audience, "This is your democracy—make it—protect it—pass it on."

He, too, had much that he could not have known at the time. Like the fact that almost forty years later, in that same town, a violent mob of young white men would rally against the progress made by Black Americans like himself and Jewish Americans like Einstein. It seemed Marshall's legal victories were the crowd running down the street and the country's culture was the straggler in the back, angry and in denial about how much had changed. It was a new round of an old fight, and the job was not finished.

Marshall ushered forth consequential legal victories with such consistency and over so many years that the late civil rights icon and Georgia representative, John Lewis, once remarked that Marshall "must be considered the founding father of the New America." There was no denying that the work of justice remained eternally unfinished but, as a result of him, the future *would* look different.

Like the classic comment about greatness, which suggests that everything before it becomes obsolete and everything after bears its imprint, Marshall's legal victories left a clear and indelible mark on how society and institutions are structured. With all he accomplished for so many people over so many years, how was it that Marshall wanted to be remembered? As a legal lion? A civil rights leader? Trailblazing Supreme Court justice? Nothing so grandiose, it turned out.

Considering the question, Marshall answered simply, "He did what he could with what he had."

And now, with all we have inherited, it is our turn to do the same.

TRUST IN THE LONG ARC

Ambiguity as Acceptance

> One must wait until the evening
> To see how splendid the day has been.
>
> — SOPHOCLES

It was around Sundays, with their "bright bedclothes" and "wrapper of no expectation," that the renowned poet Gwendolyn Brooks centered one of her most enduring love stories. But it was on a Tuesday morning that the Pulitzer Prize-winning Brooks stood in a civic center square in Chicago with fifty thousand people circled around her. Twelve hundred square feet of light blue fabric lay draped over a 162-ton sculpture behind her. What the public art piece looked like and what it meant were still unknown. But why this sculpture came to be in Chicago with so many people waiting for its reveal was already clear.

Four years earlier, in 1963, an architect named William Hartmann traveled to the French Riviera. He was carrying a collection of Chicago-themed memorabilia. In the assortment were models of the midwestern city and photographs of notable figures. Later, he shipped even more items he considered inspiring, like jerseys from local sports teams and a fireman's helmet.

Hartmann's firm was designing the civic center and hoped to boost its profile with a large-scale public sculpture created by Pablo Picasso. To make it happen, Hartmann had to sell the inscrutable, world-famous artist on the wonders of Chicago, a city the eighty-one-year-old Picasso had never visited and, likely, never would. At the same time, Hartmann had to convey to Picasso how badly Chicago was in need of someone so noteworthy to elevate its standing in people's minds.

So, along with the pride-of-the-city gifts, Hartmann presented the artist with a poem describing the midwestern city as "a place waiting for a spirit." The idea was that Picasso could be that spirit. Chicago wanted—*needed*, some would say—his fame, as though being associated with the name alone might suddenly endow Chicagoans with a prestige and legitimacy that had always evaded them.

On that Tuesday morning in August 1967, Hartmann found himself standing in the civic center with his plan realized. A small grouping of potted flowers sat near his feet. Next to him was Chicago's mayor, who held a long cord attached to the massive blue covering. Everyone there knew that beneath it stood a sculpture designed by one of the most famous people in the world, and they were ready for it to take them to the next level.

TRUST IN THE LONG ARC

When the cord was pulled and the cover finally came down, the crowd's hope for a better tomorrow came down with it. The five-story-tall sculpture stood exposed before the people for the first time and they didn't like what they saw. They didn't like its bizarre shape or its beady little eyes. They didn't like that it was so big and odd. Most of all, the crowd didn't like that they couldn't even tell what it was.

The sculpture was immediately described as everything from a giant insect to a greedy slumlord. Maybe it was a woman? A dog? A baboon? "Wings of justice," as the mayor had claimed? *What was it?*

No one knew for sure and, short of reaching this most basic level of certainty, many Chicagoans felt that the city had been played. Some even believed Picasso had pulled a prank on the city, that he had orchestrated the whole occasion as an elaborate joke. This object that was supposed to make the world take them seriously turned out to be just another reason for the world not to.

It was Gwendolyn Brooks who seemed to most anticipate the piece's poor reception. She, perhaps more than any person gathered that day, *knew* Chicago. She saw the city's people for who and how they were. With poetic prescience, Brooks cut through the day's pretensions.

The first line of the poem she wrote for the unveiling read: "Does man like Art? Man visits Art but squirms."

For all that the mayor wanted the Picasso to do for the city, in the end, he could offer only reserved confidence. In his

AMBIGUITY IS THE ANSWER

speech, he told the gathered crowd the sculpture was being dedicated "with the belief that what is strange to us today will be familiar tomorrow." In essence, he was admitting that he knew the piece was weird, and he wouldn't try to convince anyone he loved it or even understood it. He simply hoped that, in the future, others might see something in the piece that he and the crowd gathered that day clearly did not.

It's worth asking, how often do we treat ourselves with the same level of faith? How comfortable are we committing to work that might be misunderstood for some time, but we feel is the right way to go? How willing are we to see the expected path yet choose another one?

Like the Chicagoans who wanted the Picasso sculpture to immediately vault them to new heights, we can also find ourselves getting caught up in the rush for recognition. Our social feedback loops can goad us into valuing instant satisfaction over long-term impact, and have us contorting ourselves into the versions of ourselves that give us the quickest or surest bursts of admiration. It's a kind of perpetual chase of approval that is unsustainable.

The great Maya Angelou once summed up her approach to praise as: "I don't pick it up, and I don't lay it down."

She explained that while it might feel great to be told that we are amazing and important and special, if we believe people when they tell us those things then we have to also believe them when they tell us that we are none of them, that we lost what talent we once had and now are nothing.

TRUST IN THE LONG ARC

In other words, Angelou understood, the crowd is an unreliable source of esteem. It won't sustain us through the hard times or carry us over the long term.

While we might all desire recognition for our work, the goal must go beyond being *known*. We have to ask ourselves, *If we're going to be known, what will it be for? What are we truly bringing to the table?*

As well known and idolized as so many of the figures discussed in this book are today, this was not the case for most of their lives. It isn't that the myths of who they were grew over the years. It's that the extent of their contributions took time to be fully realized. Their legacies grew as people began to grasp how much the world truly changed because of their work.

The people profiled in this book mended relationships between nations and devised new strategies for social movements. They revolutionized science and forever transformed the arts. They reached the heights of sports excellence and gave people new ways of succeeding in the face of powerful headwinds.

Yet it took *time* for the world to embrace these people. It took time for others to understand the depths of what they did and the extent to which they changed the world. It took time to decide if they were something special or not. Along the way, especially in their most difficult moments, these people had to trust in the long arc of their lives. They had to believe that, taken as a whole, their impact would someday be undeniable.

AMBIGUITY IS THE ANSWER

"We live in deeds, not years," the classic Philip James Bailey poem reminds us.

One thing we learn about people who embrace ambiguity is that there is always more to them than meets the eye. There are even more deeds than it seems. Their range is even wider. Stories come out years later that make them only more incomparable in the annals of history.

Most of the time, digging deeper into people lessens our wonder for them. The brilliant image we had of them inevitably becomes marred by the flaws that were kept from us. But those who embrace ambiguity often manage to do two things at once. They give us something amazing to hold onto—artistic brilliance or world-changing insights, for instance—while also holding back. They might keep us from learning about their roles in major events or ever letting on to how they succeeded against the odds. Whatever the case may be, learning more about them only *adds to their legacy.*

In our image-conscious culture, the things we share with others tend to lean heavily toward the positive. This inevitably leaves the unsaid parts to be more negative than people's perceptions of who we are. Our dirty secrets. The truly messy and difficult moments. The things we want to keep hidden. But what if it didn't have to be that way?

What if some of the parts we kept quiet about were our finest, most impactful work? Which acts, left unsaid and unpromoted today, were they to be uncovered and explored, would lend even more credence to the kind of people we were on this Earth? How will the deeds we leave behind enhance our legacies even further?

Instead of aiming for acceptance and celebration at every step, we must trust in the long arc of our lives to produce a body of work that is meaningful. A collection that is not perfect or constantly optimized to the crowd, but stands on its own as something special.

In designing the Chicago plaza, the architects had much easier options at their disposal than a major sculpture that was, as one observer put it, "calculated to baffle the mind." They could've opted to put up monuments to the same old war heroes and politicians. They could've included an artwork that was smaller and more literal, something capable of providing a more predictable reception. Instead, they went with the route with no guarantees, and there's something to be said for doing so.

To embrace ambiguity is to accept the possibility of misinterpretation. And so it requires a certain level of faith and resistance, a willingness to be realistic about the pitfalls yet remain undeterred. To see the likelihood of disappointment and frustration in the near term yet acting accordingly because on a further horizon we see something different.

As Zora Neale Hurston observed, "There are years that ask questions and years that answer."

Twenty years after the Chicago Picasso's unveiling, Gwendolyn Brooks was again asked to write a poem in the sculpture's

AMBIGUITY IS THE ANSWER

honor. The question of what that sculpture was remained, but answers as to its impact were starting to come to light. The first stanza of her poem reads:

Set,
seasoned,
sardonic still,
I continue royal among you.
I astonish you still.
You never knew what I am.
That did not matter and does not.

Now, more than fifty years since the installation was first exposed to the world, the sculpture remains as ambiguous as ever. Woman? Baboon? Giant insect? We still don't know exactly what it was meant to be, yet people have fallen in love with the sculpture anyway.

Children climb up its base and slide down. Workers eat their lunches nearby. Artists sketch its shadows. Skateboarders sneak in tricks on it before security can catch them. There is a certain playful magic in the piece that has grown on the city. It invites us to ask questions, to wonder, and simply to be confused and amazed all at once. The sculpture remains, as Brooks later called it, "a mind extender."

The Chicago Picasso was impactful without being understood. On top of the daily wonder it engenders, the sculpture also helped usher in a movement for public sculpture that's

TRUST IN THE LONG ARC

enjoyed by millions of people every year and has gone on to partially define a new era of Chicago. It's as though this sculpture, by not being so easily grasped, helped the city lighten up a little bit and appreciate that a little ambiguity could go a long way.

Maybe it was okay to love something that couldn't be fully understood. Maybe this ambiguous object got it just right and no one could really explain why. Maybe that was fine. Maybe that was the way it had to be.

Legacies are built on more than people's initial reaction. As important as first impressions may be, our impact results from the cumulative effect of our choices, including those many actions that go overlooked or remain misunderstood. Our task is not to answer every question or clear up every confusion. It is simply to move in such a way that, when the long arc of our lives is consulted, there can be no doubt about the impact we made along the way.

CONFLICT COMES
Ambiguity as Tension

> To learn which questions are unanswerable, and not to answer them: this skill is most needful in times of stress and darkness.
>
> — URSULA K. LE GUIN

It was at the Christopher Street subway station in New York City's West Village that Jane Jacobs stepped out of her train, climbed up the stairs to street level, and fell in love with the city. She was eighteen at the time, in that stage of life when days consist of little more than searching for a job and finding cheap ways to run around town. In all her budget explorations, nowhere resonated so immediately and completely as life off of that subway stop.

Jacobs never forgot the feeling. She soon moved into an old house nearby. The world of street activity and loose community connections in the neighborhood helped her see city life in a new way. It also formed the foundation of her landmark book on urban design, *The Death and Life of Great American Cities*.

CONFLICT COMES

Rather than proposing grandiose theories or utopian plans for how cities were supposed to work, Jacobs drew her insights from observing how well they *actually* worked. She liked watching as people cut new paths across lawns, and how community members shared the responsibility for kids playing on sidewalks. She paid attention to the formal gathering places that went unused and the ways people built communities in overlooked spaces, which she saw as the lifeblood of cities.

The story of Jacobs being awed by a subway stop helps us understand her passion for city life and why she marveled at the world the way she did. But it also fits a familiar formula. The idea that, in order to accomplish anything great, we need to land on the right form of inspiration, to be in the right place at the right time. It might be a handy story, but it's woefully incomplete. Because months before Jacobs was awed by Christopher Street, the city gave her something even more valuable than inspiration: the awareness that *conflict comes*, whether we're looking for it or not.

Jacobs learned this lesson while strolling through the city's Fur District in 1935. The Great Depression was still in effect, but one wouldn't know it by taking in the scene there. Window mannequins were draped in expensive furs, and women of means bought them with ease. The stores and sidewalks were bustling with the money and ambiance of high fashion, as though the glossy pages of *Vogue* had come to life before her very eyes.

After taking in the glamor of the scene, Jacobs decided to stroll through the alleyways behind the stores. There, she chat-

AMBIGUITY IS THE ANSWER

ted with purveyors and watched as trucks were unloaded and deals were made. Like many young people, she found herself expecting public appearances to match private realities. She thought the friendly scene she saw in the stores would carry over into every other part of the business.

Yet it was there, where others failed to venture, that Jacobs began to put the picture together. Just beneath the surface, that seemingly perfect little world was teeming with conflict and competition. The straightforward act of buying and selling was crawling with antagonism. What should have been mutually beneficial partnerships were tense and full of moves to gain the upper hand. Good deals went bad, and people undercut one another with any bit of leverage they could gain.

"Each packet of furs, in its journey from trapper to fur-farmer, to auctioneer to dresser, stirs up feuds," she observed.

The Fur District taught Jacobs that the absence of conflict should not be assumed in the face of a healthy veneer. This realization was more helpful than heartbreaking. Because as much as people marvel at how inspired she was by life off the Christopher Street stop, it was this lesson in the Fur District that truly enabled her to make an impact despite all of the powerful opposition she would face. Conflict will come. It can erupt out of seemingly minor stakes and friendly relationships, even at times and in places we would not expect. She never forgot it.

The road from inspiration to impact can be a rough one and we don't have to seek out conflict along the way for it to find

CONFLICT COMES

us. As much as we might want to believe that conflict is only the bastion of certain toxic individuals, the truth is conflict is always a possibility. It can come when we're making mistakes or when we're succeeding, when we're working with others or minding our business. It's a lesson one didn't need to leave Christopher Street to learn.

During the 1920s, queer visibility had expanded significantly in the United States, especially in parts of New York City. But the resulting conservative onslaught of the 1930s and on, including increased police harassment of queer gathering places and the federal government's vicious campaign to find and punish people who were gay, forced a new level of conflict into every corner of queer life. Simply living your life could mean violence, arrest, and unemployment. And it was deliberately designed to be that way.

By the time of the Stonewall Riots in 1969, which also occurred on Christopher Street, queer people across the country had been navigating and resisting a state-sanctioned campaign against them for decades. In this onslaught, the piers along the Hudson River, just blocks from the Christopher Street subway stop, became a home for many queer people of color. There, for decades, they vogued, loved, lounged, decorated, and created in community. Some were personally cared for by the trans activists and all-around icons Marsha P. Johnson and Sylvia Rivera. Others visited for a break from keeping up appearances in their lives elsewhere, as well as for a chance to see others living with a freedom they desired for themselves.

AMBIGUITY IS THE ANSWER

This history embodies Brittney Cooper's claim that "hope and lament are not a house divided." Celebration, critique, and caretaking can connect organically. From a conflict not of their making, the Christopher Street Pier community remade their world and built cultural forms that are still embedded throughout our lives today, decades later.

It can be tempting at times to think that it's possible to avoid conflict entirely, that there's some "right" way for us to act that will allow people to get behind us and stay on our side. If we live how others tell us to live. Move how they tell us to move. Wait as long as they tell us to wait. The Christopher Street Pier community reminds us there is no behavior one can enact that will steer us clear of conflict entirely. There is no dance, no perfect sense of decorum, we can adhere to that will satisfy everyone. Conflict comes, and thinking it won't only sets us up to be unprepared for when it, inevitably, rushes in.

Of course, most of the time we're not caught up in anything. And when our lives are not racked by strife, it can be hard to empathize with those whose are. It's easier to assume that something flawed about others makes their predicaments inevitable for them. Somehow they had it coming. Clearly, they brought it on themselves.

The subtext of such thinking is clear: We don't expect to be in their same situation.

That's why it's helpful to remember that individual traits aren't always responsible for producing conflict. Certain shifting dynamics are especially prone. When someone is moving faster or more successfully than others anticipated. When someone feels their position slipping. Or a previously equal arrangement starts becoming lopsided. When these shifts start, small acts have the potential to be viewed not as isolated incidents but as claims on the future, as attempts to define and solidify what tomorrow will look like. Accordingly, as the sociologist Roger Gould discovered, the ambiguity that emerges in these moments breeds conflict.

After all, competitive dynamics are not physics. Actions and reactions are almost never equal. The same behavior can feel inconsequential to one side and existential to the other, which is why the historian Michael Howard believed that conflict was especially likely in cases of "a great power which sees itself declining to the second rank."

The issue is not that we will always be going up against some great power, reigning over everything the sun touches. Rather, it is that the people we cross paths with while doing our work may be inclined to believe that for their slice of the world—their industry, their neighborhood, their department—they are, in Howard's words, a great power. And so they will fight hard to preserve that position.

Mark Suster has lived through this many times while helping small companies go up against established, dominant players. In 2017, it happened once more when a startup in his firm's portfolio awoke to an aggressive lawsuit from the leader in their industry.

The small company's leaders were wracked with fear over

how the situation could derail their progress. How much time and money would fighting the lawsuit cost them? What would it mean for raising funds or hiring new employees? What other landmines might be lurking in their future?

It was easy to feel overwhelmed by the pressures of the moment but Suster didn't get frustrated when the lawsuit came. He didn't focus on how unfair or unfounded it felt. He didn't act frantically or let his thoughts spiral out of control. Instead, Suster was sanguine. He had been preparing for this moment for years.

Suster explained, "Once somebody realizes that your business has a strong chance of taking food off of their table, their first reaction is to grab for the knife." Recognizing that competitive dynamics rather than individual traits were responsible, he called the situation "tragically predictable."

In the years before the lawsuit, Suster encouraged the startup to use an overlooked growth strategy. Rather than charge forward loudly, they moved quickly yet quietly. Even in Los Angeles, where the company was founded, their success often went unnoticed. While other companies chased headlines, they moved like the trees of Birnam Wood in Shakespeare's *Macbeth*, capturing valuable ground without being noticed.

By virtue of trying to transform an industry, Suster knew conflict would come sooner or later. The goal was to avoid stirring up ire prematurely, so the startup could be in a position to defend itself when the attacks eventually came.

Knowing those who had never lived through such a moment

CONFLICT COMES

might be scared of what it meant, Suster gathered the organization's leadership team together. This wasn't the end of the road, he told them. The lawsuit wasn't a stain on the company. They wouldn't be crushed. In fact, it was a turning point.

"We finally know we are winning," he said.

This wasn't a delusional pep talk. It was true. By this point, the startup had made enormous progress. They could take a few hits from the traditional industry leader and still be alright. In fact, the startup had made so much progress that it was acquired less than a year later for what was rumored to be a billion dollars.

At its core, ambiguity is the acceptance that alternative futures are possible. Today's dynamic might not be tomorrow's. Those on the top might fall. Those at the bottom might climb. The result of these shifts is an ambiguity that holds no guarantee the future will be the same as the past.

Jane Jacobs knew that once the possibility of a new dynamic arises, conflict often comes. Having never graduated from college, she was attacked as illegitimate by those with credentials. As a woman challenging the approaches of male-dominated fields, she had her ideas ridiculed and dismissed. And as someone who saw things differently than those who came before her, and cared enough to fight for her ideas to be heard, she was no stranger to having a target on her back.

Someone was always salty. Someone was always sniping about this part of her work or that part of her life. Jacobs knew she was under no obligation to respond to everyone. She had

AMBIGUITY IS THE ANSWER

to let many things go, and leave a lot of attacks unanswered. But that didn't mean she avoided conflict at all costs.

Just because we do something often doesn't mean we must always. Jacobs knew that there are times when ignoring a situation is the wrong approach. Some conflicts need us to do more than look good on the sidelines. They demand our attention and ask us to concern ourselves with a purpose bigger than our comfort. It can be hard to do this when we expect to fail. After all, "Nobody likes to practice futility," said Jacobs.

She's right. It's hard to put up a fight when we expect to lose. But we must not be so fearful of confrontation that we shirk away at its first showing. If we're going to be in the arena, then let's truly be in it. Conflict is one of the costs of showing up. We have to accept it and keep going.

In a way, we all start out as the wide-eyed transplant to the big city, stepping out of the subway, marveling at the world around us and the potential it holds. The place where a lot of us struggle is right after that point, when we try to take our place at the next level of our lives. We see where we want to be and the changes we want to usher in, but we struggle to actually do it. We try and are shot down. Or we get started and can't handle how much more resistance and skepticism and embarrassment there is than we expected.

When Jacobs wrote *The Death and Life of Great American Cities*, she foresaw the conflict that would come. She knew whose expertise and positions of power she was calling into question. She knew how they would take her words and all the things they would say about her. So there was no point in sugarcoating what she was doing.

Her very first sentence reads, "This book is an attack on current city planning and rebuilding."

A much younger Jacobs might have hoped to propose new ideas and not have people view them as attacks on their success. By this point, she knew better. If she wanted to put forth new ideas, then she had to anticipate the conflicts they would engender. She would expect to be met with controversy instead of unanimous acceptance.

This approach served her well throughout her life. For instance, when Jacobs and her fellow organizers faced off with the infamous power broker Robert Moses over his plan to destroy Washington Square Park by running a highway through the middle of it, she was sober in her analysis. She knew that the man who wielded unchecked power over New York City for forty years was capable of doing anything to get what he wanted. She didn't hold an unrealistic belief that Moses would walk away, or that because they were trying to preserve something good, they deserved to win.

Instead, Jacobs recognized that they were in a battle with power. And so she told her fellow organizers their job was to make their opponents "feel like they're being nibbled to death by ducks." They listened, and deployed everything they could think of against Moses until they succeeded against the man who had been unbeatable so many times before.

Though Jacobs is remembered as a fighter, she did not set

out to be one. In fact, she saw conflicts like the battle over Washington Square Park as intrusions on the relaxing life she wanted to live—reading, writing, and spending time with friends. But, just like for those at the Christopher Street Pier, moments of conflict found her anyway. And, just like them, she didn't use the fact that she wasn't looking for conflict keep her from doing what the moment asked of her.

When we believe that conflict is only for those who have bad aims, we handcuff ourselves in the face of those who can do real harm. Jacobs demonstrated that we can fight like hell *and* maintain the moral high ground. We can stand up for people *and* win. Even if our opponent has always won. Even if those around us feel daunted by the task. Even if we're unsure ourselves.

Conflicts will come. The only thing we control is whether we'll navigate them successfully, with our morals and character intact, or not.

WHEN THE METRICS DON'T MATCH

Ambiguity as Split

> The world changes according to the way people see it, and if you alter, even by a millimeter, the way a person looks or people look at reality, then you can change it.
>
> — JAMES BALDWIN

The day Charles Darwin had been waiting for finally arrived. After half a lifetime of work collecting and analyzing specimens from around the world, he sat in his study holding a beautifully written explanation of evolution. It was clear-eyed and convincing. In less than ten handwritten pages, this little essay summed up the powerful ideas and revelations that had been swirling around Darwin's head for years. It was all there.

We might expect Darwin to feel a sense of satisfaction as he read through the essay. Maybe relief or a sense of completion. Instead, a sublime anxiety took hold of him. And the reason was simple: Charles Darwin didn't write the essay on evolution he was holding. In fact, he hadn't published on evolution at all.

AMBIGUITY IS THE ANSWER

Up until that moment, Darwin believed he was the only person in the world tying together disparate details of natural history into a generalizable theory of adaptation. He had spent years conducting experiments, reading an impressive range of topics, and corresponding with scientists all around the globe. He couldn't fathom that anyone might arrive at the same conclusion without doing everything he had done.

Yet there it was.

The essay arrived in the mail from Ternate. It was written and sent by a man named Alfred Russel Wallace. He and Darwin had corresponded before though they never met, having maintained something of a symbiotic relationship from afar. Wallace gathered new specimens during his travels in distant places and Darwin purchased them. The setup funded Wallace's travels and allowed Darwin to amass an impressive collection for studying without leaving his home. In opening Wallace's package from Ternate, Darwin most likely expected to find it contained some new specimen. Instead, he found his life's work laid out in someone else's pen.

"I never saw a more striking coincidence," Darwin wrote, stunned.

The initial shock was bad but, as with an earthquake, there was even more to come. Wallace asked Darwin to pass along the essay to one of his most prominent friends. Logistically, it was an easy task. Emotionally, it was a bit more difficult. Passing along Wallace's piece was the equivalent of Darwin giving up his right to claim evolution as his own.

WHEN THE METRICS DON'T MATCH

Darwin was a respected figure but it isn't hard to imagine that he might have, at least momentarily, considered all of his options upon hearing the request. Ternate to Down House, where he lived, was more than seven thousand miles. Perhaps Darwin could pretend as though he never received the essay? Maybe he could hold it in his study until he published his own article on the topic? Just about every option, from the upstanding to the unjust, probably crossed his mind.

Who deserved to claim evolution as their own idea was a complicated affair. Darwin came to understand the idea slowly over time. He had communicated with others about it but never shared his views formally in writing. Wallace hit upon evolution in a flash of insight while he was sick, and had now shared his argument in print. Both people could easily make a case for why they were right but it wouldn't necessarily settle the score. After all, there was no perfect way to determine who the theory belonged to, no single metric they could use to decide the matter.

These kinds of moments can do us in. When we invest so much of ourselves in our work, we hope some kind of payday or prestige will come our way. And the closer we are to having it—or having it taken away from us—the more we clamber to grab it. But this temptation can be resisted. Rather than allowing these moments to ruin our relationships, we can use them to strengthen our connections. We can see them as opportunities to carry ourselves in the best way possible precisely when we might be tempted to do the opposite.

AMBIGUITY IS THE ANSWER

For all that was at stake over the discovery of evolution, Darwin and Wallace could've spent their energy fighting and tearing one another down. Frankly, as so many others do, they could have bickered until the end of their lives. Instead, Darwin and Wallace saw it as an opportunity to do right by one another.

Darwin passed along Wallace's essay to his friend, just as he was asked. And a year later, when *On the Origin of Species* was published, Darwin praised Wallace in the book's second paragraph for separately coming to such a monumental conclusion and inducing Darwin to publish what quickly became one of the most influential books of all time. And, in fact, it was Wallace who encouraged Darwin to use the phrase "survival of the fittest" in later editions of *Origin*.

These two were caught in a moment with high stakes and no easy answer, and handled it with grace. Though much of the fame accrued to Darwin, he made sure to provide Wallace access to new professional circles, and arranged for him to receive a pension for his major contributions to science. Darwin even remarked later in life that of everyone invoking his name, Wallace was the only one who truly understood what he was saying. Words of praise flowed freely between the two throughout their lives.

This is not to say that either man was passive. (They weren't.) Or that they didn't each push hard for themselves. (They did.) Rather, Darwin and Wallace understood that, in the midst of

WHEN THE METRICS DON'T MATCH

fundamentally changing people's minds, claims over the idea of evolution were a distraction. The real task was revolutionizing how people understood their world.

Introducing a perspective that radically upends someone's worldview, as Darwin and Wallace were doing, often results in a split being created in people's minds between what was and what else might be. What was singular and certain suddenly becomes ambiguous and unknown.

We give too little credence to how painful and difficult this process can be. People rarely swing from one way of seeing to another in an instant and we need to stop acting as if they will. Each of us is a web of assumptions and beliefs, value judgments, and biases. None of us lets go of major parts of ourselves overnight, and that's okay. No crisp line divides a meadow from a forest. There is always overlap, always a liminal zone, which transitions us from where we were to where we're going.

To present a new way of seeing is to introduce ambiguity. It is to ask someone to live in the forest and the meadow at the same time. To hold two interpretations simultaneously and, for some time, not know which is best. In this sense, the success of producing ambiguity is that it makes way for a fuller acceptance tomorrow.

The secret is to anticipate people being resistant. Expect it to be difficult for others to reconcile their current thinking with what is proposed, not because they are weak or lazy or unwilling to adapt but because, if we are pushing revolutionary

AMBIGUITY IS THE ANSWER

new ideas, there won't be a shared metric by which someone can weigh the paths against each other. There won't be some simple calculation to guarantee which way forward is best.

In the philosopher Thomas Kuhn's seminal book on major shifts in knowledge systems, *The Structure of Scientific Revolutions*, he proposed the idea that new and old bodies of knowledge can be "incommensurable" with one another. That is to say, they might make perfect sense within the context of themselves but comparisons between them are unworkable. The situation becomes ambiguous because there is no way to reconcile the alternative paths. They are fundamentally different explanations of the same phenomenon. Rather than being able to calculate a clear winner, people are presented with a split between possibilities and forced to choose.

At the heart of Kuhn's argument is the idea that worldviews are worlds unto themselves, supported by coteries with their own sources and shorthand. It's why we often talk past one another and struggle to reach a shared understanding of even common terms. We can look at the same phenomenon and each see something entirely different.

Our ways of making sense of the world don't go away quickly or quietly. "Neither problems nor puzzles yield often to the first attack," Kuhn explained. And so we might have to put a new vision in people's laps. Instead of swinging them all the way to a new way of seeing, it might simply be our responsibility to create a split where there once was only a flawed certainty.

There is no guarantee we will be successful. But producing

WHEN THE METRICS DON'T MATCH

a split in people's minds where there once was certainty is a critical step in creating change. It means the way they had seen the world isn't necessarily the way it is. It was potentially only a vantage point, a lens. The same phenomenon might mean something very different when seen through a new worldview.

Kuhn was particularly impressed by the extent to which Darwin seemed to be at peace with the ambiguity-ridden nature of change. Having begun *On the Origin of Species* with praise for Wallace, Darwin ended the revolutionary book, which has never been out of print since its first publication, with an acknowledgment of what he was up against, and how unbothered he was with the task before him:

> *Although I am fully convinced of the truth of the views given in this volume…I by no means expect to convince experienced naturalists whose minds are stocked with a multitude of facts all viewed, during a long course of years, from a point of view directly opposite to mine.*

With such a revolutionary idea in their hands, Darwin and Wallace surely wanted to see their work change people's minds about the world. But they didn't expect, or even seem to desire, the immediate affirmations so many people cling to in determining their worth. Instead, they possessed a presentiment of people's resistance. They knew that even after putting forth such comprehensive and convincing arguments for evolution, many people would continue taking comfort in the metrics and mindsets they were used to, and refuse to be swayed. Instead of

AMBIGUITY IS THE ANSWER

looking for a quick grasp or a settled score, Darwin and Wallace looked to the next generation to carry their work the distance it was always meant to travel.

Likewise, we can't let the fact people are reluctant to move a millimeter prevent us from trying to move them a mile. Some times and circumstances call for revolutionary, rather than incremental, change. If what is being ushered in is significant enough, it will produce a split in people's understanding that opens up new possibilities and spurs a new set of inquiries.

To arouse a question is a victory in itself.

RETREAT AND RISE

Ambiguity as Options

>They will not know I have gone away to come back.
>
>— SANDRA CISNEROS

For all the talk of how much things have changed, sometimes it feels like the way things are has been the ways things are for too long. With so much to be reimagined and done differently, it seems like we can never be moving too fast. This only makes the setbacks and delays we inevitably experience feel worse. They're the wrong thing at exactly the wrong time, no matter when they occur.

But these unwanted interruptions can do more than just frustrate us and slow us down. They can provide us with options that point us in new, better directions, even if it means having to backtrack a bit. After all, there is something about a retreat that can get us to where we're meant to be. And no one understood this better than the great Mexican artist Frida Kahlo.

AMBIGUITY IS THE ANSWER

Today, she is one of the most iconic faces in the world. Her colorful self-portraits, replete with indigenous clothing and androgynous embodiments, are recognized as a unique depiction of beauty, pain, and strength. She was the first Latin American artist to garner more than a million dollars for a single work of art. More importantly, Kahlo remains an icon to millions of people who turn to her work as a source of inspiration, representation, and power.

Always a rebellious yet diligent soul, Kahlo attended what was considered to be the most prestigious high school in Mexico, where she loved socializing with peers from across a wide range of groups. Even at a young age, she had a clear picture of what she wanted to become and was studying hard to make it happen. Painting wasn't part of the plan. Kahlo was studying to become a doctor.

Then one day she was riding a bus in Mexico City like she often did and, out of nowhere, a streetcar crashed into her bus and smashed it against a building. People were thrown from the vehicles and screaming in pain. Kahlo was among them, hemorrhaging on the sidewalk, with a metal handrail impaled through her pelvis. The first doctors who operated on her, when she was finally taken to a hospital, expected her to die.

Kahlo survived but was left bedridden and isolated for months. Suddenly, instead of becoming a doctor, she was relying on them. And with her family unable to afford the medical bills, Kahlo ended up dropping out of school. Eventually, her

RETREAT AND RISE

friends moved on and stopped visiting so often. The pain and loneliness of her bedridden existence were unbearable.

Up until then, Kahlo had put herself on the most promising path she could find. Now, through an accident entirely out of her control, she was in a much worse place than where she started. Kahlo was forced to endure chronic pain that would bother her for the rest of her life, and to retreat from the path she wanted so badly. Stuck at home, she gave up on her dream of becoming a doctor.

Jolted so far off her path, Kahlo was unsure how to move forward again. And so, simply to get through the upheaval, she began to paint. Using a special easel and a mirror installed by her mother above the bed, Kahlo spent her days painting what would become her most meaningful subject: herself.

Initially, it was simply a way for her to pass the time. Then, she found that selling the occasional painting was a helpful way to contribute sorely needed funds to the family's finances. Over time, as Kahlo painted more and considered seriously focusing on this new path, she sought perspective. Was she onto something or was she fooling herself? She wanted to know.

Having recently met the Mexican muralist Diego Rivera at a party, she visited him while he was working on a new piece nearby. Rivera was high up on a scaffold when Kahlo arrived holding a stack of paintings in her arms. Unintimidated, she told him to climb down and assess her work, and to be honest.

AMBIGUITY IS THE ANSWER

"I want an absolutely straightforward opinion because I cannot afford to go on just to appease my vanity," she explained.

Kahlo knew how badly we can want to be told our approach is right, and how important it is to not deceive ourselves. *Don't let me fool myself*, she seemed to be saying. Kahlo had already needed to retreat from her dreams of practicing medicine. If she needed to do the same with art, she would.

Yet how often do we go on, as Kahlo said, just to appease our vanity? How often does a fear of backtracking keep us from moving in a better way? How often do we miss our path because we're too committed to the one we're already on?

As counterintuitive as it seems, it is often retreats out of the limelight that help us go farther. Retreats help us see with fresh eyes. They give us perspective and create new opportunities. Retreats buy us time and expose the errors in our plans. They allow us to regain our strength for the long-haul and focus on what matters most.

If modern life teaches us anything, it is that we get *a lot* out of being seen, recognized, and valued. Stepping back and being out of the hustle of everyday life can be difficult. Even the most intrinsically driven of us yearn for validation. We have a need to know that our time and presence are helpful. To leave the feedback cycles we're used to, even for brief periods of time, can be a struggle. To be away from what we are used to is *hard*.

But how can we reflect on our lives if we won't step back from them long enough to reassess our options? What's going to happen if our response to every situation is to plow forward no matter what? How much time will we waste working on the wrong things? How many terrible plans will we see through to completion?

Some people make success look as easy as walking through a grocery store gathering accolades but, back in our own lives, progress is typically frustrating and slower than expected. It's a slog. A few promising steps forward always seem to be followed by another shove backward. We put our heads down and keep marching, only to bump into a new set of problems. Stepping away from the action in these times feels wrong, like proof alone that we don't have what it takes to succeed.

It can be hard to see the delays and obstacles we face as anything but annoying interruptions. Hassles. Errands. Tasks. *Things that need to be dealt with.* We want them over and out of our way so we can keep marching down the paths we're on. But, like Kahlo realized after her accident, a new setback shouldn't be an excuse to fall back on old ways. In fact, it might be exactly what we need to move differently.

The physicist and astronomer Galileo Galilei shared Kahlo's knack for appreciating the potential in a retreat. The man who supposedly said that nobody was so ignorant that he couldn't learn something from them seemed to hold the same enviable attitude about experiences. And it was good that he did.

Galileo was instrumental in laying siege to the idea that humans were the center of the universe. Building on the work of Nicolas Copernicus, he argued for a heliocentric under-

AMBIGUITY IS THE ANSWER

standing of the world, the idea that the Earth rotates every day and orbits around the Sun. Instead of the universe revolving around us, as centuries of belief had taught, we were simply one piece of the cosmos.

Galileo helped usher in one of history's most significant revolutions of human understanding. But as these things tend to go sometimes, rather than receiving praise and recognition, he was arrested. Galileo was convicted of suspected heresy and forced to recant his arguments. The teaching and distribution of his most impactful work became prohibited. And, as even further punishment, he was sentenced to live out the remainder of his life on house arrest.

Even so, Galileo understood that his situation could have been worse. A fate of physical and intellectual retreat was much better than the death sentence he could have easily received. Still, Galileo's fall was a mighty one for a person who had gone up against doctrine and pushed human knowledge so far forward. Didn't he want to double down on his claims instead of backing away? Shouldn't he have wanted vindication and to be given his due? Not necessarily.

Galileo took the life change in stride. He accepted his new downgraded social position and set himself to studying a different set of subjects. There was more to learn and, out of the eye of the public, Galileo began one of his most productive phases. Forbidden from looking to the stars, he dove into work on seemingly more neutral topics about how material conditions are changed.

RETREAT AND RISE

For instance, he wanted to know why objects break at certain points but not before. What does it take for those first cracks to begin to form? How does something finally burst through its constraints? How much pressure is too much?

It surely wasn't Galileo's life goal to be sentenced to house arrest studying the resistance of ropes and rods. But in challenging doctrine and powerful institutions, he understood what he was up against. It was a difficult yet sober assessment. He knew how strong and entrenched people's beliefs can be, and the difficulty of changing minds. He understood that people resist new ideas, and that those in power always have an incentive to stifle change. Rather than accomplish everything he sought to do overnight, he knew he would need to entrust some of his impact to time. After all, pressure has to build before it can break through.

Aspects of Galileo's story are appealing, like the idea of still being remembered nearly four centuries later. So, too, is his willingness to risk so much in support of his views. But what about all the other parts? The way he had to backtrack so far? The fact that so much of his life's work was tarnished, discredited, and banned? What are we to make of those pieces?

People often celebrate those who were bold in the face of every obstacle and fought until their last breath, but that doesn't make it the right approach for all situations. Galileo reminds us that we need to reserve the right to be discerning about what's worthy of our focus. Barreling ahead no matter what can waste our time and energy on fights that don't deserve us.

Nearly two thousand years before Galileo was sentenced to house arrest, and hundreds more before Frida Kahlo began painting, the philosopher Socrates stood barefoot in a public square. He had earned a reputation for dissecting big and small concepts with anyone he could rope into a dialogue. On this particular day, he struck up a conversation on the concept of *courage* with an Athenian general named Laches. To ensure the two of them were starting on the same page, the philosopher asked the general to define the virtue.

"Good heavens, Socrates, there is no difficulty about that," said Laches. "If a man is willing to remain at his post and to defend himself against the enemy without running away, then you may rest assured that he is a man of courage."

All these years later, Laches' definition seems to hold up. Courage, we all know, requires facing adversity head on, not running away. Courageous people stand up and cowards back down. If we want to be seen as courageous, we can't run or hide from difficult situations. We have to be willing to fight through them. We have to keep marching forward. Right?

Despite its apparent logic, Socrates didn't buy the argument. If courage is a willingness to stand and fight, he said, what are we to make of someone who retreats out of a bad situation? Is it really courageous to fight every time one is provoked? For our purposes, is that really how we want to define what Maya Angelou called "the most important of all the virtues"?

In many ways, we still live with the ghost of Laches' definition. However, there's no reason to see courage and retreat as antagonistic to one another. Rather than a headstrong march forward, courage is often demonstrated by a willingness to learn and adjust, to be flexible as our knowledge and circumstances change.

Angelou described it as the willingness to say to others that you have learned a new truth and were willing "to change your way of thinking."

Putting it simply, Kurt Vonnegut wrote that "a step backward, after making a wrong turn, is a step in the right direction."

They each knew what Frida Kahlo and Socrates knew: Any idiot can mindlessly march forward. Anyone can be so obsessed with how they are seen and the path they are on that they end up taking better options off the table.

The last thing any of us need is to march into disaster because we didn't give ourselves the option not to. Rather than fall into familiar tendencies, we have to give ourselves the space to make better decisions. We need to learn to act based on what a situation demands of us, not on how we moved yesterday or on how we hope to be seen. The ancient Chinese strategist Sun-Tzu described this as aiming to be one "who advances without coveting fame and retreats without fearing disgrace."

Some moments demand reflection. Some obstacles can't be bulldozed. Some paths don't deserve to be marched down. We need to give ourselves the freedom to be dynamic. Rather than a rigid commitment to being courageous in the Laches sense, we need to be capable of being both bold and mindful, of advancing and retreating and continually finding better options.

AMBIGUITY IS THE ANSWER

To do so, we have to resist being boxed in by past approaches, even if they served us well. It is in the retreat from rigid conceptions of ourselves that we discover new ways of moving ahead. We give ourselves access to new ways of being in, and moving through, the world. New skills. New mindsets. New lines of inquiry and ways of working. New possibilities.

In Ralph Ellison's powerful novel *Invisible Man*, the protagonist's retreat came after a wealth of experiences. He had been full of promise and celebrated early on for the great things he would accomplish in life. He had been praised and afforded new levels of access. He had given speeches and led his community. In a real way, he had been many people's hope for what was possible.

But the climb to influence was not straightforward. He had also been used. He had been played and attacked, set up, demeaned, manipulated. The high points of his life were contingent, as they too often are, on playing a role that others demanded of him. So he stepped away.

He moved to an illuminated room beneath the city where he spent his days listening to Louis Armstrong records while treating himself to a vanilla ice cream and sloe gin dessert. In time, away from the action, he began to see his life in a new light.

He saw the parts that, caught in the business of others' expectations and his own drive for acceptance, had been unseeable before. He saw how foolish he had been, just as he began to see the actions of others with the harshness they deserved.

He began to realize how others had nudged him in the wrong directions and twisted his skills and mannerisms into forms they could benefit from.

Seeing anew was difficult but necessary work. Everything wasn't as straightforward as it felt in the moment. Retreating helped open his eyes and change his perspective. But, while the time away was a helpful and much needed reprieve, he knew it couldn't last forever. No retreat can or is meant to.

As Ellison put it, "hibernation is a covert preparation for a more overt action."

The world is always there calling us to rise to the occasion once more, to take what we have learned away from the eyes of others and tap back in in a new way. There comes a time when we must again claim our place in the context of history.

It wasn't only the action that Kahlo and Galileo and Ellison's narrator stepped away from. It was simplistic versions of themselves that were no longer helpful. They had to discard the old straightforward definitions in order to come back ambiguous and anew.

Don't buy the idea that successful people are going nonstop. Don't worry about the myth of perpetual progress or the expectation that we remain constantly busy. The truth is others are constantly moving away from old versions of themselves, and retreating from paths that made them successful but won't take them any further. We have to be just as willing to find those parts of ourselves that need to be walked away from, so we can recognize what we need next. If we're unwilling to retreat from flawed paths when we're on them, we'll prove ourselves to be no different than Laches' general who marches into trouble simply out of fear of turning around and going a new way.

Think about it this way: A retreat is not there as an excuse to run away when things get hard. It is about making sure that, in every situation, we aren't marching forward with a version of ourselves that isn't needed, even if it served us well in the past. A retreat should help us take the new skills and perspective we developed out of the limelight and *make use of them*.

The purpose of a retreat is to rise anew.

METABOLIZE MOMENTS

Ambiguity as Interpretation

> I try not to find the form too soon. Instead, I try to think about it as an idea without a shape.
>
> — MAYA LIN

The cool waters of the Pacific Ocean are only about a hundred miles west of Delano, California, but, in many respects, they're a world away. Located in the southernmost county of the San Joaquin Valley, Delano is an agricultural town. One of those places on the map known mainly by those who live there and those who left.

Sixty years ago, Delano was even more remote and overlooked. People kept their heads down, struggled to get by, and little ever changed. Like a lot of places, Delano was trapped in that most addicting of all facades, convinced that the way things were was the way they were going to remain.

That bubble burst on September 8, 1965, when Larry Itliong helped keep more than a thousand Filipino American farm

AMBIGUITY IS THE ANSWER

workers out of the grape fields on strike. The next day, the number doubled to more than two thousand. The workers' ask was far from exorbitant: They wanted to be paid $1.40 per hour plus $0.25 per box of picked grapes.

The growers balked. They felt a well-founded confidence that they could avoid making any concessions to the farm workers. The growers' wealth, political capital, and close connections to the police made them nearly untouchable. They *ran* Delano, and had little interest in seeing the town's balance of power shift away from them. Plus, they knew the law was on their side.

The landmark labor legislation of the 1930s, the National Labor Relations Act, which provided a host of new protections for workers, explicitly excluded farm workers. The people who made sure the country had food to eat were singled out and denied the same recourses provided to just about anyone else who worked. To put it simply, one of the biggest leaps forward for workers leapt over farm workers entirely.

This left growers free to wantonly exploit their workers, and many did. Physical and sexual violence were not uncommon. Wages were plundered. Workers toiling under the hot sun were barely given water, and it was usually filthy when they were. Planes caked the fields and the people who worked them in dangerous pesticides.

One of the growers' favorite tactics for keeping workers vulnerable was to separate people of different ethnicities and play them against each other. Itliong refused to let it to happen again. At his urging, about a week after the Filipinos left the

METABOLIZE MOMENTS

fields, they were joined by over 1,200 Mexican American farm workers. These were members of the nascent National Farm Workers Association, co-founded by Dolores Huerta and Cesar Chavez. The group voted overwhelmingly to support the strike, even though they weren't particularly ready to undertake one. Underfunded and moved to act before they were fully prepared, they joined anyway.

"Nobody exactly knew what was going to happen," said Huerta.

In many ways, *this* is how turning points actually come about. We have one idea of when a moment will play out, but circumstances force us to act much sooner. We strive to be ready, but the moment calls for us before we actually are. We haven't raised enough money or mapped out all of our steps, yet still we must step forward and act.

The moments that change the world almost always crop up at unexpected times and places. They show up unannounced, banging on our conscience. They may be on difficult timetables and riskier than we would like. And though they come with no guarantees of success, they require us anyway.

If there is a skill worth having, it is to see what any moment can do for us. Audre Lorde referred to this as the ability "to metabolize experience, good or ill, into something that is useful, lasting, effective." We have to be able to make something new out of whatever we've been given, to see in every moment something more than what it looks like initially.

This isn't as easy as it might sound. Our minds are moti-

AMBIGUITY IS THE ANSWER

vated to make unmerited simplifications. They shut the door to alternatives so fast we don't even realize it happens. And in exchange for the answer that comes to us most easily, we give up all the other potential interpretations.

"Instead of a rich definition of the situation, reality may become reduced to a thin party line," explained the sociologist Erving Goffman.

To put it another way, we see certainty when we should be seeing ambiguity. So we have to push our perception further than our minds want to go on their own. We have to remind ourselves to interpret the world as *more ambiguous* than our instinct tells us. We have to keep the door open to interpretations that are more useful than our initial read of the moment.

Ask: How else can this moment be put to use? What would change the dynamic? What's being overlooked by everyone else?

These were exactly the kinds of questions a man named Lee Sedol was asking himself in 2016, while sitting at a table in a hotel in Seoul, South Korea. He was surrounded by video cameras and a small crowd. In a moment that held echoes of Garry Kasparov's famous chess matches against Deep Blue in the 1990s, Lee was playing the ancient board game Go against an artificial intelligence computer program.

Developed at least 2,500 years ago, Go is the oldest board game in the world still played in its original form. Though simple in its structure—two sides use stones to capture space on a board—it is far more complex than chess. According to

METABOLIZE MOMENTS

researchers, a game of Go can play out in more ways than there are atoms in the known universe.

Lee is one of the best to ever play the game. He achieved the rare 9 dan rank and has won eighteen international titles. In fact, this is why he was chosen to play. The makers of AlphaGo, the computer program, wanted to see if it was capable of beating the best. So far it had been. AlphaGo won the first three matches.

Lee was seventy-seven moves into the fourth game when he was trying to interpret the board in a new way. He was at a clear disadvantage and knew it. His soft eyes searched the board intensely, assessing and reassessing his options. His left hand rubbed the back of his neck. Tens of millions of people around the world watched his every gesture. Every option available looked futile.

As the pressure grew, one of the commentators told viewers, "Lee Sedol needs to do something special. Otherwise, it's just not going to be enough."

Then, in a simple act with a profound effect, he placed a stone on the board that changed the game's entire calculus. AlphaGo's probability of winning, which was calculated continuously and had been squarely in its favor throughout the match, plummeted. Lee's move 78 seemed to throw the computer into total disarray. It made a series of subsequent mistakes. Before long, AlphaGo had dug itself into a hole it could not escape from and was forced to resign. *The human beat the computer.*

AMBIGUITY IS THE ANSWER

Move 78 is remembered in the Go community as the "hand of God" and, with it, Lee Sedol carved a path to victory out of what looked like a dead end. At move 78, the board presented Lee with what looked like a no-win situation. He had many options available to him but they all seemed to spell eventual defeat. But Lee saw something else. He looked at the same board with stones arranged in the same manner and interpreted it differently than everyone else. He saw an opportunity they all missed. One move possessed the potential to fundamentally restructure the dynamic, and Lee found it.

Remember, how we interpret the world affects how we navigate it. In our own work, we will be presented with moments where we must see new possibilities, as unlikely as they are, where no one else sees them. From people's certainty of disappointment, we will have to help them see the prospect of victory.

Back in Delano, the Filipino and Mexican farm workers turned bad situations into something good over and over. They weren't just playing up the positives to soothe their fears or make themselves feel better. They were proving that what a moment meant, what one could make of one's circumstance, was open to interpretation. Events that seemed to have only one meaning were shown, time after time, to be more ambiguous and useful than expected.

Cesar Chavez was a master of such moves. When he was at his best, Chavez could turn any moment into momentum for the movement. He seemed to have a sixth sense for knowing when an event had the potential to derail the farm workers'

METABOLIZE MOMENTS

cause, and possessed a unique ability to transform the moment into something *useful*.

Throughout the strike, Delano growers tried stifling the farm workers' effort. One example, early on, occurred when a grower-friendly sheriff warned that workers weren't allowed to say *huelga/welga*, the Spanish and Tagalog words, respectively, for *strike*. The initial read of the moment was that this was a clear setback. In it, however, Chavez saw an opportunity.

He gathered a group of predominantly women supporters. He also gathered the press. Naturally, the police showed up as well. When the supporters started chanting *huelga/welga*, they were promptly arrested, with the press on hand to capture the scene of women being put in handcuffs simply for using their voice. In a tight encapsulation, the moment revealed and helped disseminate an awareness of how power was being deployed against farm workers in Delano. It was also turned into a fundraising opportunity that very night.

Opposition to the farm workers didn't always come in legal forms. Among other forms of attack, the growers sprayed striking farm workers with sulfur fertilizer and forced their cars off the road. These wicked tactics made it almost impossible to speak to those still going to work in the vineyards. Undeterred, Chavez took to the sky. He rigged his friend's Cessna airplane with a public announcement system and spoke directly to the workers from the air.

At the beginning, the issues between the farm workers and the growers were constrained to Delano. The town was

AMBIGUITY IS THE ANSWER

awash in clashes. At the vineyard entrances. Inside the courts. Outside the jails. Delano was *the* place. Both sides knew the local advantages weighed heavily in favor of the growers if it stayed that way.

Like Lee Sedol, Chavez needed to look at a situation where the odds were stacked against his cause and interpret the conditions differently. He needed to find a move that could restructure the nature of the conflict and provide an opportunity to win. He needed to do something special or else the farm workers would fail.

It was at this moment, when everything was heating up in Delano, that Chavez did something nobody saw coming. *He left.* He literally walked away.

Chavez organized some fifty farm workers to march out of Delano and onto the highway, headed north, away from the action. The group didn't march for a mile, or an hour, or even an afternoon. Instead, it was a pilgrimage, more than three hundred miles from Delano to Sacramento, through dozens of towns. Chavez ingeniously choreographed political and religious symbolism around the march. They carried U.S. flags, and signs with the farm worker eagle and images of the Virgin of Guadalupe. The group arrived in the state capital on Easter Sunday to a cheering crowd of more than eight thousand people.

The Delano growers might have expected to keep the whole affair a simple, local issue—that is where they had the most power, after all—but those days were over now. The farm workers reinterpreted a straightforward power imbalance and added new dimensions in order to make it rife with ambiguity. Suddenly, the growers had to contend with a new set of questions.

Was this a financial fight or a spiritual one? Was the farm workers' cause a local issue or a national one? Were they negotiating a contract or waging a public relations battle?

There were no easy answers, and the growers soon learned that their strengths in one area were hindrances in another. The bully tactics that worked on a local level were strategic nightmares on the national level. So the farm workers continued to reorient the fight around new dimensions, creating advantages where and when it looked like they were outmatched.

The results weren't instantaneous. But after five years of relentless organizing, including Dolores Huerta's coining of the timeless rallying cry *¡Si, se puede!*, a national boycott that got around seventeen million Americans to stop buying grapes, and the involvement of everyone from priests to presidential candidates, the farm workers eventually got the growers to sign on to their demands. *They won.*

Over the course of the conflict, the farm workers had to maintain a stubborn willingness to turn hard moments into helpful ones. They repeatedly faced a political board weighted heavily to their disadvantage and interpreted it in new ways. They found moves even when it looked like there were none.

Our algorithmic world has taught us that the same inputs produce the same outputs, as though the strategic situations we find ourselves in can be reduced to simple formulas. But this isn't how the real world works. At the root of ambiguity is

AMBIGUITY IS THE ANSWER

an acceptance that the same information can produce different interpretations. Others can look at the same board with the same set of factors and see nothing but dead ends, while we see the move that opens up a path to victory.

If we give up our ability to decide what a moment means, we give up the power to determine what is possible. So we have to be willing, no matter how stacked against us the board might look, to see more than what appears at first, and much more than what others will say is there. In a world where others are better connected and have more resources, our interpretation of the moment can be our greatest advantage.

REMEMBER THE POWER OF SECRETS
Ambiguity as Protection

> If ever you are tempted to look for outside approval,
> realize that you have compromised your integrity.
> If you need a witness, be your own.
>
> — EPICTETUS

Perhaps unsurprising for someone who accomplished so much in secret, Harriet Tubman never divulged the exact details of how she escaped to freedom. What we know is that she freed herself in 1849, and her first taste of liberation was nothing short of divine.

"When I found I had crossed that line, I looked at my hands to see if I was the same person," she reflected. "There was such a glory over everything; the sun came like gold through trees, and over the fields, and I felt like I was in Heaven."

Freedom was many lifetimes overdue, and it wasn't meant only for her. So while she settled in Philadelphia, found community, and began working, the joy of that first glorious moment began to give way. Having witnessed too many false promises of freedom, she began plotting her return south. First, to free her family. Then, over the course of nearly a decade, to free hundreds of people.

Harriet Tubman was the living embodiment of Toni Morrison's belief that "the function of freedom is to free someone else."

By the time she escaped, it had been some 230 years since people were first brought to the United States and enslaved. From craftsmen creating coffles to financiers funding plantations, just about everything reinforced this most barbaric institution. For all of the lofty talk about liberty and rights, moral hypocrisies abounded, and justifications for slavery seemed to win out every time. The heartless flywheel of an economy built on terror was humming.

In 1850, less than a year after Harriet Tubman made it to Philadelphia, the country doubled down on protecting enslavers' interests. In September of that year, the U.S. Congress passed a piece of legislation known as the Fugitive Slave Law. The law expanded and enshrined enslavers' power nationally, arming them with every legal and extrajudicial weapon they might need to capture people who had liberated themselves. Not only did it increase the danger for anyone like Tubman who had taken their rightful place in this world as a free human being, but it would make it harder for others to as well.

With the risks raised to unimaginable levels, Tubman decided to dedicate her life to giving freedom to others. She made liberation a year-round orientation, aligned with the seasons.

REMEMBER THE POWER OF SECRETS

In the summer, she worked in vacation spots like Cape May, New Jersey, and saved whatever money she could to fund her travels.

In the fall, Tubman would plan out the details of the next escape she would lead and begin sending coded messages to plantations in preparation.

Many of her escapes were timed to occur in the winter, often before Christmas and, almost always, before New Year's Day.

And after leading those she had freed hundreds of miles north, Tubman would spend her springtimes in Canada with family and friends, recovering from the long journey and regaining the strength to do it all over again.

And over and over she did it.

Harriet Tubman knew something we are far too apt to forget: Actions don't require attention. We've been taught that we need to be known in order to make an impact. It has been drilled into us that without a platform, without popularity, we can't actually make a difference. And so we have produced too many people saying and doing whatever it takes to be noticed, too many people fabricating appearances.

Just because the fascination with popularity is so pervasive today doesn't mean it's the only path forward. Never mistake a mindset's ubiquity for its soundness. Attention and popularity don't always increase our ability to make an impact. Some meaningful work is easier when we aren't being watched. Sometimes masking what we're doing can allow us to work unimpeded. Flying under the radar can be a godsend.

AMBIGUITY IS THE ANSWER

If any group stands in sharp contrast to our modern addiction to public praise, it's that ambiguous network that shepherded people from slavery to freedom known as the Underground Railroad. The people involved did their most meaningful life's work in secret. They stayed quiet about contributions that changed the course of people's lives. And they took risks for something they knew they could never be recognized for fully. The Underground Railroad reminds us that for all the attention placed on public leaders, history often turns on the actions of dedicated individuals working without acclaim.

There was no room for a philosophy like "fake it 'til you make it" in work this important. You either did what it took or you didn't get involved. The participants didn't wait until they had built up audiences or reached some arbitrary level of success before being of use. They helped how and where they could, sneaking people into boats or transporting them through the night, forging train passes, cooking meals, and providing safe places to rest. They protected, instead of promoted, their life's most meaningful work.

Like freedom seekers using asafetida to cover their scent from bloodhounds, the Underground Railroad could only succeed if its participants masked each of their steps. The consequences were deadly serious for everyone involved. If the participants sought fame or recognition for their contributions, lives would be lost.

These extra precautions made it difficult for slavery's supporters to interdict the flow of people to freedom. As Eric Foner

REMEMBER THE POWER OF SECRETS

pointed out, city leaders often "found it impossible to discover the names of those who assisted fugitives." Following a series of escapes, the editorial board of one Virginia newspaper asked with frustration, "Is there no way to break up this 'railroad'?"

Increasingly, the answer was no. The Underground Railroad was too ambiguous, too full of deception and misdirection, to be stopped.

Divulging our plans in a dangerous climate is rarely helpful. So the Underground Railroad's participants had to work in what the historian Stephanie Camp called "the wide terrain between consent, on one hand, and open, organized opposition, on the other." They used an ambiguous design to protect the overall network and the individuals involved. Families turned their homes into base camps that could not be detected. Messages of great importance were coded into everyday items. Even common scenes, like funerals, were staged in order to usher people out of town, hidden inside coffins.

Every day, without calling attention to what was happening, this ambiguity kept people flowing to freedom. Every day, this ambiguity kept the network intact a little longer.

The historian Robert Caro once made the enduring observation that power doesn't so much corrupt people as *reveal* who they truly are. It shows us what they've always wanted and how they really feel about others. And the reason, Caro said, is that as one gains power, "camouflage is less necessary."

While that may be obvious—who hasn't marveled at what the powerful are able to do in the open?—the related takeaway

AMBIGUITY IS THE ANSWER

is key: Camouflage is a fact of life when we're at a disadvantage. For Tubman and the other participants in the Underground Railroad, secrecy, camouflage, and ambiguity were matters of life and death. The 1850 Fugitive Slave Law directed the full apparatus of slaveholding power at ending their impact. And yet, through ambiguous design, those involved in the Underground Railroad continued ushering people to freedom.

Crumbling systems are often presaged by their story falling apart. Escapes were simultaneously liberation and attacks on the nation's narrative. They destroyed the myth of enslaver omnipotence and proved that there were holes in the system. Each person who took back their freedom served as a glaring reminder that the end of the enslavers' reign was being plotted and executed under their noses without detection.

Formerly enslaved people made their influence felt another way as well. They forced white northerners to contend with the realities of slavery, to recognize that it was not an issue divorced from their lives but, in fact, a moral crisis in which they were bound up as well. Those who successfully escaped showed up on the doorsteps of northern communities to tell their stories and show their scars, to make visceral what was abstract, and to prompt action where there was indifference. Their impact only grew with the start of the Civil War.

Using the same strategies developed over the years to facilitate escapes, people fled from plantations to Union lines from the beginning of the war. They showed up expecting to be taken in, and to contribute to the effort. But the white Union

REMEMBER THE POWER OF SECRETS

commanders possessed an utterly flawed understanding of slavery's dynamics. They believed the mythology that enslaved people were loyal to their enslavers, and were convinced that formerly enslaved people would also be loyal to the Confederacy. So rather than taking them in, Union forces did the most appalling thing they could have done: *They took those who had escaped back to their enslavers.*

For Harriet Tubman, this was devastating and beyond infuriating. Now working as a Union nurse in Port Royal, South Carolina, she argued that freeing enslaved people would be key for winning the war. And she set out to prove it.

After developing a spy network of Black Americans that scouted out conditions behind enemy lines—a land to which the white troops wouldn't venture or fully understand—she confirmed that those trapped by slavery were eager to join the Union effort. There was only one caveat: Enslaved men wanted guarantees that their wives and children would be free and safe. As it had been for her, family was of utmost importance to them.

With guarantees in place and covert logistics mapped out with precision, Tubman was ready to act. On the night of June 2, 1863, she led 150 Black troops traveling on boats up the Combahee River. Tipped off in advance that the river was stocked with explosives meant to prevent such an operation, the boats successfully maneuvered through the water without incident. As the boats began reaching the plantations, the troops noticed figures waiting for them along the riverbank.

AMBIGUITY IS THE ANSWER

There were hundreds and hundreds of people gathered at the water's edge to, finally, get free.

Under Tubman's leadership, the soldiers burned and raided nine plantations over the course of the night. They hit each one in such quick succession that the enslavers were unable to usher a significant defense. Amid the chaos, enslavers called out to those they had terrorized day after day to come to their defense. They begged. They pleaded. But it did not matter. By the time the enslavers grasped that their violent rule of human lives was crumbling around them, it was too late. In a single night, the Combahee River Raid freed more than 750 people.

The official Confederate report on the raid acknowledged how thoroughly surprised and outmaneuvered they had been. They had *no idea* it was coming, which is another way of saying that the days leading up to the raid were more ambiguous than they seemed. Under the guise of business as usual, something else entirely had gone on without detection.

The Combahee River Raid was a major demonstration of the soundness of Tubman's thinking. Before the raid, enslaved people provided invaluable intelligence. And once they were at Union forts, they continued contributing significantly to the war effort. In fact, the eventual addition of formerly enslaved people to the Union side was a major turning point in the Civil War. Not only did it provide a host of new strengths, but it also eliminated the possibility that their skills would be forced into use by the Confederacy.

REMEMBER THE POWER OF SECRETS

Of course, the white Union leaders didn't come by this realization of their own accord. They were reluctant participants. But those who escaped from slavery forced the issue into their laps. Had it not been for people risking everything to escape, along with a history of skills and strategies to make them successful, the Union might have never brought formerly enslaved people into their ranks, or won the war.

In 1868, the great abolitionist Frederick Douglass wrote a letter to Tubman. In it, he sang her praises and acknowledged how much she had done without "the applause of the crowd." As if summoning the ancient philosopher Epictetus, whose quote introduced this chapter, Douglass told Tubman that, in some ways, "'*God bless you*' has been your only reward. The midnight sky and the silent stars have been the witnesses of your devotion to freedom and of your heroism."

We have enough people seeking the applause of the crowd above all else. What's in short supply are people who will do what needs to be done, whether or not anyone is there to witness the part they played.

LOVE YOUR LAYERS
Ambiguity as Completeness

> How to explain, in a culture frantic for resolution, that sometimes the shit stays messy?
>
> — MAGGIE NELSON

Imagine, for a moment, that it's 1970. We're standing in a public market in Vietnam, in what was then called Saigon. People are bumping into one another as they make their way through the crowd. The smell of spices and hot cooking oil hangs in the air. On sellers' tables and carts sit just about anything someone might hope to buy.

A wiry man in tan khaki pants and a short-sleeved white button-up shirt looks at a selection of birds. His name is Pham Xuan An, and he scans the mix of canaries and parrots, skylarks, owls, and pheasants. Then he moves to a different area, where he looks with a little less interest.

An older woman named Nguyen Thi Ba ambles up to him while he's smoking a cigarette. They make small talk about the nearby animals and, after a few minutes of polite conversation, An notices how destitute she looks. He reaches into his bag and hands Ba a package of paper-wrapped meat rolls, called *nem chua*. She is deeply appreciative and hands him something in return. At this, he reveals an easy, charming smile. Then he tells her he needs to get to work, and politely excuses himself.

An heads to the office but, in truth, he's already completed his most important task of the day. Now it's Ba who has her work cut out for her. She needs to carry the meat rolls from Saigon to Soc Mon without being captured. If she makes it, she'll transfer the package to another courier, who will take them even farther north to Cu Chi.

Twelve years his senior, nondescript and always chewing betel nut, Ba was handpicked by An. They worked together in this way for fifteen years, transferring packages and barely speaking. In the words of one historian, they were "truly one of the oddest and most effective espionage teams in history."

As tasty as the *nem chua* may be, their flavor pales in importance to the paper wrapped around them. On this, An has written a message in invisible ink made of rice soaked in water. Ba doesn't know what it says. But she does know that it was written by one of the most important people in Vietnam.

In Cu Chi, the meat rolls will enter a maze of underground tunnels and eventually be given to someone cleared to read messages of utmost secrecy. To do so, they will pour an iodine solution over the paper and learn, for the first time, what it

AMBIGUITY IS THE ANSWER

says. An's reports are often long and detailed. But this one was short and direct:

> *An American journalist was recently captured who once put himself at great risk to save the lives of Vietnamese children in Cambodia. If he's still alive, then he must be released immediately. No questions asked.*

The journalist's name was Robert Sam Anson, and he was still in the custody of the North Vietnamese. In fact, he had spent two weeks enduring a grueling interrogation, and there were no signs life was going to get any better or end well for him. His wife and employer had both been notified of his disappearance, but they had no idea how to find or free him. The fate of other journalists who'd recently died surely weighed on everyone's mind.

Then, suddenly, Anson was released and no one, including him, had any idea how it happened.

The truth would not come out for many years, though it was quite simple: Anson was saved by a note wrapped around some meat rolls, simply because it was written by a wiry man named Pham Xuan An.

An lived in a Vietnam forced to deal with the motives of outside interests. First, it was Japan. Then the French. And then the United States. His home was used as a proxy for issues that had nothing to do with Vietnam itself. These were not circumstances of his choosing. He didn't opt in to such precarity. Instead, it was thrust upon him. And, as a result, An was forced to make a way for himself, to carve an expansive and impactful life out of unthinkable conditions.

Likewise, none of us are asked if the time and space in which we live works for us, if the treatment we receive is what we wanted. Nobody makes sure we'll have the strength to deal with what we're faced with, or if we're going to be able to navigate the contradictions and deal with the gut-wrenching trade-offs we're, at times, forced to make. The time and space we occupy is much bigger than us, and the vast majority of it is beyond our control.

There will always be barriers. Hard moments sometimes pile up all at once. Danger and difficulty can cut into life just when things are going well. There come times when we must make impossible choices, where every option has downsides and nothing feels good or is guaranteed.

With the tensions of today, it can feel like now is precisely the time to pick sides. But history is full of contentious times, and the temptation to entrench ourselves is no stronger today than it was in Vietnam during the war. We're always being asked to draw battle lines, to pick our team. But An shows us that, when everyone else is screaming and waving their battle flags, there can be a certain unparalleled power in a more ambiguous approach. To understand why, we need to better understand An.

An was a cornerstone of life in Saigon. He could usually be found in café Givral, telling stories and laughing, almost always with his German shepherd at his feet. He was said to

AMBIGUITY IS THE ANSWER

understand the Americans better than any other Vietnamese person, and the Vietnamese better than any American. He was funny, well connected, and extremely insightful. For instance, when asked to explain the importance of some current event, as he often was, An would usually begin his answer with a history lesson beginning in the fifteenth century. He seemed to know everyone and be everywhere, yet his life was far more ambiguous than anyone realized at the time.

To American journalists and Vietnamese government officials, An was often the most helpful person in the room. He had the best sources, and was almost always the first to know when a significant event just occurred. His insights were also unmatched. An was constantly being asked to read and provide analysis on new strategies and reports. His assessments were detailed and honest, which made him trustworthy and brought him into even more rooms. In fact, An was so close to high-ranking officials for the South Vietnamese and United States governments that, for a time, he was in charge of teaching their spies how to maintain cover and avoid getting caught.

There was more though.

At the same time that An was training spies for the South, he was spying for the North. He worked with Ba to send the same detailed analyses to Hanoi that he provided to his colleagues in Saigon. An also ended up playing a singular role in two of the most significant political turning points in the war, the Battle at Ap Bac in 1963 (where he rendered a major new counterinsurgency plan instantly useless) and the Tet Offensive

LOVE YOUR LAYERS

in 1968 (where he helped identify strategic targets). By the time Robert Sam Anson was captured in 1970, An's impact was undeniable on multiple sides, even if each only saw one layer of who he was.

This is part of the reason why Viet Thanh Nguyen was thinking a lot about the complex life of Pham Xuan An while writing his Pulitzer Prize-winning debut novel, *The Sympathizer*. The book's unnamed main character, in all his depth and contradictions, is loosely based on An, which gave Viet the ability to explore someone with a full range of layers. Rather than recoiling from such a character, readers were entranced and understanding. They saw someone who was not perfect or neatly packaged and, so, was actually quite human.

In a sentiment An would've surely loved, the novel's narrator remarks that "the best kind of truth" is one that means "at least two things." That is, an ambiguous one.

Asked once what the truth was about which side of the war he worked for, An replied: "The truth? Which truth? One truth is that for 10 years I was a staff correspondent for *Time* magazine and before that Reuters. The other truth is that I joined the movement in 1944 and in one way or another have been part of it ever since. Two truths...both truths are true."

An's overarching purpose was to get the United States out of Vietnam so his country would be able to determine the nature of its future for itself. And yet he spent most of his time developing and enjoying friendships with Americans. They talked for hours, pored over notes, and shared what they knew. They cracked each other up with jokes and took care of each other. He knew their spouses and played with their children. And Anson wasn't the only beneficiary of An's influence. On more than one occasion, he saved the lives of Americans, including in the final hours of the war, helping to get friends and family on the last helicopters out of the country.

An, who was loved for just one part of who he was, was terrified the other parts of his life would be uncovered. What would his friends make of the other things he had done? How would learning about his many layers change their view of him? He could only wonder.

The layers of our own lives may not be nearly as consequential as those of An's but many of us resist revealing our full character for the very same reasons. We worry how people will respond when they know more about us. We fear people will be unsupportive or disappointed when they learn that we're not only as they saw us. We hold back because we don't want to lose what we've built with others. Some part of us doesn't want to disrupt the neat little narrative people have about us.

We can end up putting so much energy into packaging ourselves that we forget about the depths of who we really are. Instead of editing out the layers, hold tight to them. Know that there will be times when we'll have to say to others: *I am more than what you saw. I did and overcame more than you ever knew.*

There is no guarantee everyone will understand the complete story. Even some of the people closest to us may not fully realize how much we've done, what we went through, or how it made us who we are today. Like the inquiry about which side An worked for, sometimes simple questions don't have simple answers.

Ambiguity often results from letting in new information. Rather than supplanting an existing story with a new one, we're asked to see what was and what is newly revealed at the same time. The essence of ambiguity is a resistance to making rigid what should be irreducible.

The innovative filmmaker Trinh T. Minh-ha has referred to this unwillingness to package culture, and by extension ourselves, as a means of "keeping alive." It's a way of saying that there's *life* in what moves beyond our instruments and perceptions. In what doesn't line up neatly. In what remains ungraspable. Ambiguity prompts an unknowing we must learn to be comfortable with, even enjoy; the humbling awareness that we only ever get glimpses and so much occurs beyond what we perceive.

It's easy to imagine how angry and frustrated An's friends might have felt upon learning that he was working as a spy the whole time they knew each other. But that isn't what happened. It turned out that even spying couldn't erode the strength of those friendships and the bonds that had been made.

An's friends came to accept that it would be naive to believe they knew the full story all along. Rather than replace their history, the new information augmented it. The new details were added to everything they knew about An, what he had done for them, and the many times he went out of his way to help people who, theoretically, he should have been against.

AMBIGUITY IS THE ANSWER

"I can only say with certainty that on the last day of the war he helped to save the life of a man who strongly opposed the goals that An secretly worked toward most of his life," explained one friend. "I will always remember An for that."

The writer David Halberstam, who gave special thanks to An in *The Making of a Quagmire*, was asked if he held a grudge against his old friend. He didn't: "It is a story full of intrigue, smoke, and mirrors, but I still think fondly of An."

Halberstam's feelings were representative of nearly every one of An's old friends. They seemed to understand that he was in a position of unimaginable complexity, and he balanced the cross-currents of life in Vietnam during the war as successfully as any person might. In a similar situation, we can only wonder how we would act, how we might craft a useful role for ourselves. And if An could receive such an understanding response to the fact he was a spy, of all things, then perhaps in our own small battles to love our layers, we too might be met with a grace that exceeds our expectations.

Though Anson and colleagues may have been shocked to learn another truth about An, they were also admittedly impressed. After all, for all of their analyses and reports, for all of their revamped military strategies and high-placed government officials, Americans never seemed to grasp Vietnam.

One friend of An's likened life there during the war to Salvador Dali's painting of clocks melting in the desert, *La persistencia de la memoria*. Americans were constantly duped by

LOVE YOUR LAYERS

their own certainty, and the more they looked, the more firm and final they tried to make their sense of the world, the more ambiguous every detail became. Pham Xuan An was one more glaring example of everything they got wrong.

As another old colleague of An's said, he "is a reminder to me of how much I saw of Vietnam but how little I understood."

The ambiguity Pham Xuan An embodied enabled Vietnam to accomplish two nearly impossible geopolitical goals: He helped force an occupying military out of his country *and* supported long-term reconciliation between the two sides. There was no playbook for doing all of this and, yet, he accomplished it. In the annals of history, An stands in a class of his own, having used his ambiguity to make him as impactful as any of us could ever hope to be.

"So it was that a great change came through the back door," wrote Nguyen Khai.

As for Robert Sam Anson, seventeen years after he was freed from capture, he took a trip back to Vietnam, to what is now Ho Chi Minh City. At the top of his to-do list was a reunion with An. It would be the first time the two men saw each other since Anson learned that An was responsible for freeing him.

Anson was anxious walking up to the house. After all, it was because of An that he was even still alive. Once inside, An put him at ease quickly, just like he always had, remembering family members by name and asking how each were doing. They

AMBIGUITY IS THE ANSWER

caught up on each other's lives and, eventually, the conversation reached the point where Anson could express his appreciation for all that An had done for him. But there was a lingering question still on Anson's mind as he looked across at the person who had saved his life.

"But why?" Anson asked. "We were on different sides, you and I."

"No," An replied, "we were friends."

NOISE IN THE SILENCE

Ambiguity as Connection

And there are those who have the truth within them, but they tell it not in words.

— KHALIL GIBRAN

Muhammad Ali was larger-than-life. As an athlete and activist, he was flashy and outspoken, creative and powerful. Perfectly embodied in his timeless aphorism—*Float like a butterfly, sting like a bee*—was his ability to somehow do it all. But the bravado he's remembered for made it easy to overlook an important element of his success. Part of Ali's greatness was that he kept some of his magic hidden. After all, the second part of his famous saying gets recalled far less often: *The hands can't hit what the eyes can't see.*

Despite his enormous persona, Ali made sure his opponents had no way to see or hit the most important parts of him. These were the things that, as he said, the eyes can't see. The strategies he never revealed. The intensity of his training when no one

AMBIGUITY IS THE ANSWER

was looking. The mental work he did to remain unflappable in big moments. Ali made himself harder to compete against by developing assets that were unknown to the other side. Fixated on the flashy parts, they would miss everything he did in the spaces between.

Today, Ali's name brings to mind words like *the greatest* but, back in 1974, it was starting to seem like his best days were behind him. Ali was thirty-two years old and attempting to make a comeback, having been banned from professional boxing for three years because he opposed the U.S. war in Vietnam.

The opponent he chose next was the most difficult one he could've picked. George Foreman was the current heavyweight champion of the world. And, at twenty-five years old, Foreman was the younger and much more powerful athlete. He was also the 4:1 favorite to win.

The match between Ali and Foreman was billed as the "Rumble in the Jungle," and took place in a sold out arena in Kinshasa, Zaire (now the Democratic Republic of the Congo). It was an enormous event, preceded by a music festival, and watched by an estimated one billion people around the world. To make it easier for the global audience to watch live, the match began around 4:00 AM local time. Despite the early hour, the air inside the arena was hot and thick with humidity. A storm was on the way.

Both boxers began the match by being aggressive, but a new pattern quickly emerged. They would start each round by squaring off in the middle of the ring and then Foreman would force Ali against the ropes on the ring's perimeter. Foreman looked in control, while Ali looked tired and on othe defensive. Leaning against the ropes is often a precursor to the end.

"Get off the ropes, Ali!" yelled his trainer, but it didn't change anything.

Round after round continued this way and, for fans of Ali, it was an embarrassing display. They expected him to take charge of the situation. They wanted pride and greatness and daring. They wanted to see him triumph. Instead, they got an exhausted icon on his last leg, barely putting up a fight.

By the seventh round, Foreman was ready to end the match for good. He mustered all of his energy to hit Ali with a hard punch to the jaw, and he thought it might be enough to send Ali to the canvas. But, once more, Ali leaned against the ropes and took the punch. Then, Ali grabbed Foreman and whispered into his ear, "That all you got, George?"

Foreman was stunned. He had been punching Ali almost nonstop the entire fight. Every signal he received told him he was in control and dominating. Yet here was Ali, in the moment he was supposed to fall, notably patient, strong, and defiant.

In that moment, Foreman explained, "I realized that this ain't what I thought it was."

In the eighth round, Ali was again in that familiar place, pinned against the ropes. And again, he covered his head while Foreman punched his body. But the situation was suddenly different. Ali could feel it. Foreman had worn himself out by throwing so many punches. He was *exhausted.*

Still, Ali laid against the ropes a little longer. Then, with just twenty seconds left in the round, he went on an offensive with a force no one knew he still possessed. Nine seconds later, Foreman fell and Ali was victorious.

"The thing they said was impossible, he's done," said one television announcer, as the ring was flooded with fans.

The results spoke for themselves, but they were only the culmination of a long match in which seemingly every observer was wrong about what they saw along the way. For nearly the entire match, it *looked* like Foreman had the advantage. But Ali was doing more than people realized. By using the flexibility of the ropes to absorb the force of the punches, he was quietly guiding the match. Ali was patiently setting up the conditions that would make victory possible. It required him to look less impressive than he knew himself to be and to endure more pain than he would have liked to, but those were a small price to pay for what he wanted.

The mistake people made watching Ali is one that's made all the time. It's to bifurcate one's perception into an *either-or* reading of a situation. Either Ali fights back or he is about to lose. Either he gets off the ropes or he is out of energy. Either he is a butterfly or he is a bee. Our minds generally leave little space for both, or for all the possibilities in-between. In other words, in the brain's psychologically lazy quest to make sense of the world, it habitually fails to see the noise hidden in silence. And it's this gap between what is happening and what is *perceived* as happening that holds so much possibility.

NOISE IN THE SILENCE

As the community organizer Saul Alinsky put it, "Power is not only what you have, but what the enemy thinks you have."

Most of the time this goes the way of inflating one's bona fides, with people trying to look bigger and better and more accomplished than they are. But Ali showed us the opposite approach might be even more valuable: Being underestimated can be an indispensable asset when crafting a strategy. Many great things lie in waiting, and it is okay to be one of them. Despite the barrage of messages to the contrary, there is a power in having people count us out, and in waiting to reveal all we are capable of.

Do you think Ali loved covering up and taking all of those hits from Foreman while waiting to make his move? Of course not.

None of us like to wait our turn or bite our tongue or lick our wounds. None of us want to be seen as less than we are. Ali would've probably loved to knock out Foreman in the first round but that doesn't mean it would've been the right approach. Ali was wise enough to know that such a formidable opponent would require him to work on a longer timeline and keep some of his magic hidden along the way. We need to understand when that's the case in our own lives as well.

Historically, the ability to look at a situation over time, to see and accept the many sacrifices needed to achieve a significant result, was praised. Patience was a skill much more revered than the frantic scramble we celebrate today. That's because, in situations where we are outmatched, success often has to come

AMBIGUITY IS THE ANSWER

to fruition. There are no mad dashes here. It takes time and ambiguity to get where we want to be. Rather than launching ourselves headfirst into danger in a rush for the reward, we'll often find ourselves, like Ali, needing to weigh a number of factors and employing a variety of tactics.

Rather than embodying approaches that are purely *this* or *that*, much of what we do can be said to operate along that "wide terrain," to reposition Stephanie Camp's term, between acquiescence on the one hand and outright opposition on the other. It's this wide terrain between binaries that is the site of intelligent and expansive ambiguity. It is here that we craft and deploy the kinds of nuanced strategies difficult circumstances often demand, taking what's available to us and doing more with it than seems possible.

These approaches are what communications scholar Ralina L. Joseph described in her research on Black women and media as "strategic performances of ambiguity, carefully created constructions designed to wink at certain audiences and smile blandly in the face of others." It is *by design* that these performances don't read the same to all observers. Rather than a failure of language, the ambiguity is a deft use of its ambit. The simplistic expectations of certain audiences are employed as a wrapper for conveying complex and critical messages to others.

In this sense, strategic ambiguity can be seen as highly skilled maneuvering through environments rife with risk. Rather than laying everything out in literal terms, these performances draw

NOISE IN THE SILENCE

on the silent shorthand of communities to embed instructive sentiments into otherwise innocuous activities. To do this successfully requires not only an awareness of the potential landmines of a situation, but also an ability to find the language and context capable of communicating multiple messages to multiple audiences at the same time. It is linguistic and cultural brilliance in action.

Still, even when we are capable of it, few of us would *prefer* to navigate situations in this manner. Strategic ambiguity is something many of us both know how to use and know the complicated feelings of being able to use. This doesn't mean it's inherently isolating. Being put in positions where strategic ambiguity is even necessary can itself be a wink to our communities, as our skilled navigation of these moments makes clear how keenly aware we are of the factors at play. All too familiar with being put in these positions themselves, others can read past their literal interpretations and see them for what they really are. It's with this silent shorthand that our communities grant us the option of ambiguity when a more direct approach carries too much risk, hassle, or distraction.

This supportive interplay between community, ambiguity, and outspokenness was on full display in the fall of 2022.

After being on the air for just a single season, *Abbott Elementary*, the mockumentary-style television show about the lives of public school teachers in Philadelphia, was nominated for five Emmy Awards. And the good news didn't stop at nominations.

AMBIGUITY IS THE ANSWER

The show won for Outstanding Casting, plus the great Sheryl Lee Ralph won her first Emmy award, for her role on the show as Barbara Howard.

Ralph was so stunned when her name was announced that fellow cast members had to help usher her towards the stage. But, as she would later say, center stage is her home. Once she was there, she paused, took a breath, and began singing a powerful rendition of Dianne Reeves' song "Endangered Species." Ralph followed it with a moving speech about being loved and uplifted by people in her life. "Because when you get a Quinta Brunson in your corner..." she told the audience, and the message was clear: Being with the right people can take us places we've never been.

The evening's controversy came as Brunson, the creator, executive producer, and star of *Abbott Elementary*, won the Emmy Award for Outstanding Writing for a Comedy Series, for the show's pilot episode. Rather than congratulating her and stepping out of the frame, one of the co-presenters, Jimmy Kimmel, decided to lay motionless on the stage next to the microphone. Brunson carried on, giving a proud and appreciative acceptance speech. But many observers saw Kimmel's actions as clearly disrespectful, and the image of a white man pointlessly interrupting a Black woman's success like an attention-seeking toddler resonated all too familiarly.

By the time the Emmys were over, the online world was in an uproar over Kimmel's disrespectful behavior during Brunson's speech. Observers didn't shy away from direct language in their critiques. In what the literary theorist Valerie Smith has referred to as a Black feminist "strategy of reading simultaneity," observers had no trouble recognizing the gendered and racialized connotations of what Kimmel did. These critiques were so prominent that they were showcased in outlets like *Newsweek* and *USA Today*, and drove much of the public conversation around the moment.

The message found Kimmel offline as well. Backstage, Sheryl Lee Ralph made it clear to his face how inappropriate his actions were. "Ooh, the disrespect, Jimmy," she said.

Two days later Brunson made an appearance on Kimmel's late night show. By this point, people had made the critiques of Kimmel's behavior quite clear. The direct language of Ralph and others made it possible for Brunson to work in that ambiguous space between approving the behavior and outright opposing it. With the onus for being direct carried by the community, she was able to convey important messages to her audience while gracefully handling a dynamic rife with risk.

On the show, Kimmel apologized. In her reply, Brunson managed to accept the apology without excusing his behavior, which would have discounted the very real criticisms people voiced.

When Kimmel went on to say that his actions stole the spotlight and ruined her night, Brunson didn't affirm his framing of her evening. As if reminding him that the ability to protect her joy isn't a co-sign of his behavior, she subtly pushed back and reclaimed her experience.

AMBIGUITY IS THE ANSWER

"Honestly, I had a good night," she told him. "I had a great night! I had such a good night."

And for good reason.

Brunson won her first Emmy, for a pilot she wrote, for a show she created, with a team she cared about deeply. Some of those people *also* won Emmys. The drama of the evening wasn't of her making. And Brunson made clear what a distraction it was when she had so much more important work to do.

Reminding Kimmel of her many responsibilities with *Abbott Elementary*, she let him know that the morning after the Emmys she was right back to work with her team on the new season, which had already been extended from thirteen episodes to twenty-two. Wrapping her prolific creative output in a joke, Brunson told him, "As an actress, I'm really upset at the producer of my show for making that the case. As the producer of my show, I feel like all the actors should fall in line."

Brunson's central purpose for appearing on the show was to uplift *Abbott Elementary*. Rather than allowing the focus to shift onto Kimmel, she kept the attention on her team. She publicly celebrated their first season's success, and recognized their hard work under way on another incredible season.

Brunson was immediately praised for her handling of the controversy. And while some viewers might've seen it as a textbook public relations clean up—*Mistake, Apology, Forgiveness*—others saw in Brunson's nuanced handling of the moment a strategic performance of ambiguity that managed to, as Ralina L. Joseph put it, "wink at certain audiences and smile blandly in the face of others."

There was simply more going on than some people realized.

The same can be said of Ali as well. While it may be easy to portray him as simply leaning on the ropes and covering up, his strategy for the "Rumble in the Jungle" was far more nuanced. Like Brunson, Ali needed to do many little things with expert precision in order to accomplish the big aim he was after. He, too, had to find the right times to go with the flow and the right moments and ways to push back.

In fact, his moments on the ropes read like winks to us today. We see them not only as they appeared, but also for what they *were*. What looked like acquiescence was an intelligent and effective ambiguity capable of accomplishing an outcome the experts said couldn't be done.

KEEP MOVING
Ambiguity as Advantage

> The most effortful forms of slow thinking are those that require you to think fast.
>
> — DANIEL KAHNEMAN

Somewhere in the bowels of the Pentagon, a phone rang in a windowless office and a man named Jim Burton was given an ultimatum: *Retire or be transferred to Alaska.* He had one week to make his decision but the message was already clear: *We want you out.*

The shock was not that power would be wielded over someone like this, but that he of all people should be on the receiving end. Burton was born in Normal, Illinois. He was a self-described product of the system, and as by-the-book as they come. Conservative and white, with a lifetime of privileges, Burton's goal in life was to become a general, and he had been well on his way to achieving it. Burton attended prestigious schools, was a star athlete, and was promoted ahead of schedule. He followed the rules and the path laid out before him, and was consistently rewarded for it. The only problem was that he had now reached a point in his career where he had seen enough corruption and chicanery to know that chasing his dream any further would mean co-signing behavior he abhorred.

Burton's job was to evaluate the safety of an expensive and confusing military project called the Bradley Fighting Vehicle. What the Bradley was and why it was needed were nearly impossible to describe. This wasn't due to any classified nature, but rather because its mission and design had morphed so many times over the years that it had lost any clear purpose. The Bradley looked and moved like a tank, but was only about as safe as a bus. And, because of how it was built, when it was shot the inside filled up with deadly vapors.

Initially meant to be a troop transport vehicle, the Bradley was really the poster child for the problems of the defense industry. It was such a fiscal and militaristic mess that conservative and progressive media outlets found rare unity in their criticism, referring to it as a "dump" and a "rolling death trap." With its exaggerated capabilities and out-of-control costs, the Bradley epitomized what James Fallows called the Pentagon's "culture of procurement," the masquerade that spending more money equated to making better decisions.

The acclaimed writer Paul Beatty once wryly observed that "there's nothing to do at the Pentagon except start a war." In Burton, a host of generals found the target of theirs. For them, the goal was to get the Bradley into production as soon as

AMBIGUITY IS THE ANSWER

possible so that they could get promoted. Burton's willingness to make sure the vehicle was safe got in the way of this, so they rebuffed him at every stage of his work.

He was denied access to information he needed. His work was manipulated. And he was lied to over and over. After two difficult years in his position, Burton had managed to get himself nowhere but ostracized. And now they were trying to ship him off to Alaska.

Going against a cause we were once dedicated to almost always means that, at some point, it broke our heart. This was the case for Burton. The winks, nods, and approvals that enabled the system—what Walter Isaacson referred to at the time as the "symbiotic ties between the military and defense contractors"—didn't sit well with Burton. But that didn't mean he had any idea what to do about it.

For his part, Burton knew he was in over his head. The level of strategic thinking the situation required didn't come naturally to him. He had hoped the right path would be the easy path. Instead, he began to realize, doing the right thing would only lead to harder days ahead.

He found himself asking the evergreen questions: How do I move with integrity and still succeed? How do I see a difficult moment all the way through to completion?

One night, while contemplating his next move, Burton's good friend, John Boyd, gave him a timely piece of advice. "Jim, you may not win," he said. "But you can't give the bastards a free ride."

Boyd was a good person to have giving you advice. He had dedicated himself to understanding how those with less resources prevail over those with more. He dug through history, studying conflict all around the world, trying to find the strategic elements that allowed smaller, seemingly weaker groups to win when the odds were against them.

Boyd's landmark revelation centered around the psychological effects of producing ambiguity through movement. Rapid movements, especially if there is an unpredictable element to them, can change a competitive environment faster than others can make sense of it. The side that can't keep up begins operating under an expired sense of reality, where they are viewing new actions through an outdated understanding of the situation. In turn, the environment becomes ambiguous, making it harder and harder to take in and respond to new information appropriately, which leads to strategic missteps.

Boyd realized there's nothing inevitable about ambiguity and no reason why we must only be on its receiving end. His research demonstrated that, throughout history, one of the greatest advantages groups with less resources could create for themselves was the production of an ambiguous environment. The key is stacking actions with such a rapid pace and level of unpredictability that the other side loses an intuitive feel for where the situation is going next or why.

Conceptually, this is why the extra pass in team sports is so effective. Ball movement forces an opposing team to respond to a constantly changing environment and, if the

AMBIGUITY IS THE ANSWER

pace of the movements exceeds the team's ability to keep up with them, an ambiguous environment gets produced where it's no longer clear where the play is going next or why. The rapid movements produce ambiguity, which causes mistakes and creates opportunities.

When Steve Kerr took over as the head coach of the Golden State Warriors in 2014, he incorporated this insight into the team's strategy. His charge to the players was to pass the basketball at least three hundred times every game. In order to reach that number, they would need to keep the ball and their bodies moving.

"The main goal," explained star point guard Stephen Curry, "is to just make the defense make as many decisions as you can so that they're going to mess up at some point."

Before Kerr's ball movement plan, the Warriors hadn't been to the NBA Finals in forty years. In his first eight years coaching the team, they averaged more than three hundred passes per game every season. They were also NBA champions four times.

The mistake most of us make is not going far enough. Our metaphorical passes are too slow or we give up too soon. We never reach a tempo capable of producing ambiguity and so we never enjoy its strategic possibilities. Instead of making the metaphorical extra pass, we pause and let everyone get back into position. Having achieved a small bit of success, we pat ourselves on the back instead of continuing to push.

KEEP MOVING

We never break the threshold that gives us a real advantage. We never actually produce an ambiguity the other side must sort through.

This is what people so often get wrong about moving quickly. The point isn't to just get things done faster. It's to move in ways that interrupt the decision-making process of the other side. It's to expand the gap between our understanding of the environment and theirs. The real benefit of rapid movements in competitive environments comes from producing ambiguity the other side must contend with.

Boyd was knee-deep in research on how the seemingly powerless prevail over the powerful when Burton received his ultimatum. It was fortuitous timing. After all, what better testing ground for Boyd's strategies than a lone staffer facing down the full power of an institution?

Persistence and unpredictability make powerful partners. So Boyd was confident that if he could get Burton to keep moving, no matter what the Pentagon tried, new opportunities would arise. The key would be working at a tempo faster than the bureaucrats he was battling. This charge to keep moving wasn't license to act erratically. Burton didn't have carte blanche to do whatever he wanted. Instead, his actions were guided by clear principles. He had to work within established policies and be perfect in his research.

Burton's approach embodied an old adage: *Slow is smooth and smooth is fast*. Rather than hurting his tempo, Burton's diligence

AMBIGUITY IS THE ANSWER

kept him out of trouble and allowed him to spot opportunities that otherwise wouldn't have been apparent. From there, he could move rapidly in ways that threw off the other side. He could make wise, effective decisions no one else saw coming because he had done his homework beforehand.

For instance, when the ultimatum call came, Burton initially felt like it was the end of the road. Over the years, he had assembled a detailed and damning collection of reports, memos, and research on the vehicle's many hazards, but it wasn't enough. It seemed like the fight was over and he'd lost.

Boyd was undeterred. He saw the transfer as a mistake by the other side. He told Burton to gather every piece of evidence he'd assembled and share it with anyone who had ever been involved with the Bradley. On top of the stacks of information, Burton should add a memo updating each person on the status of the tests and of his sudden transfer to Alaska. Boyd jokingly called these stacks "little brothers and sisters." He and Burton both knew that, once distributed, they would spread through the Pentagon like kids on a sugar high.

Laughing, Boyd said, "If something needs to leak outside of the Building, God will take care of it."

Copies of Burton's reports were not only passed around the Pentagon, but also across town into the hands of staffers and officials on Capitol Hill. Then, they went farther, into the hands of reporters. What began as a small, internal matter about the testing process for a troop transporter was suddenly spilled across the headlines and editorial pages of the country's largest newspapers. Facing such public backlash, a Pentagon spokesperson denied that Burton was ever being transferred to Alaska. Once journalists realized they had been lied to by the government, it set off another wave of critical press.

This kind of cat-and-mouse chase played out over and over. Just when the bureaucrats were sure some move they made would put an end to the whole matter, they would face the sudden, often public and embarrassing, realization that they failed again. Burton might prove experts wrong in front of their superiors. Or generals would awaken to their abuses of power displayed in the media. Every time what they thought was the right move was shown to be wrong, they became less certain of the situation. They also became more cautious. And here was the real advantage: As the tempo of the other side slowed, Burton picked up his pace.

For nearly two years, Burton had been forced to respond to the pace set by others but now he and Boyd were able to flip the dynamic. They were finally moving and making decisions faster than the other side. They were producing an ambiguous environment and using it to gain new advantages.

Gates of power rarely break open on one big thrust. So, as social movement scholars Frances Fox Piven and Richard Cloward pointed out, "strategies must be pursued that escalate the momentum and impact." The energy has to build. The pressure has to increase. The surprises have to keep coming.

AMBIGUITY IS THE ANSWER

The idea is not that one act wins the day, but that momentum, once gained, never lets up. Burton would have to *keep moving*.

Though he was spied on by his own government and attacked repeatedly, Burton's willingness to keep going began to have another helpful effect. He started getting phone calls late at night from people he had never met before. Though he often felt isolated in his battle against so much power, Burton realized that others were paying attention to what was being done to him and were moved by his persistence. His callers were offering more than well wishes. They had first-hand knowledge of the ways the military sabotaged his work, and were more than happy to share information Burton could use in his fight. He wasn't alone at all.

The battle over the Bradley was one piece of major public frustration in the mid-1980s over the Pentagon's outlandish spending. People were sick of the billions of dollars in cost overruns racked up by defense contractors. They were tired of seeing their hard-earned money wasted on failure after failure and war after war. On top of everything, the public was fed up with the military's lies and excuses for why the whole system functioned so poorly, yet lined the pockets of defense contractors so successfully.

The situation became so bad that, in a town famous for never truly questioning the military, a bipartisan collection of congressional leaders banded together and called for public hearings. They decided to put a special focus on one project that exemplified every issue of concern: the Bradley.

KEEP MOVING

For days, Burton had to sit idly while a parade of generals leaned on their rank, rather than the facts, to talk up the vehicle's capabilities and defend its ballooning price tag. Then, finally, Burton was going to get his turn to speak publicly. But at 5:00 PM the night before he was set to give his testimony, he received one more unwanted phone call.

The caller informed Burton that all of his upcoming comments about the Bradley were now classified. That meant that if he said anything about the Bradley during his testimony the following day—in a hearing *about the Bradley*—he would be charged with divulging classified information to the public.

Again, he was being silenced. And again, he seemed to have no say in the matter. Power was being wielded over him once more.

Early on, Boyd had told Burton that the key to moving quickly was to always maintain the initiative. "When they surprise you, even if the surprise seems fatal, there is always a countermove," Boyd said. It was clear Burton needed one now.

He stayed up late going through the generals' testimonies and then, the next morning, he called the person back. Burton had a new plan. He was prepared to go to the hearing and use it as a forum to inform Congress and the press that, in the last twenty-four hours, his testimony had suddenly been censored by the U.S. Army. And then he was prepared to detail exactly how and when some of the Army generals had revealed classified information in prior days during their own public testimonies.

AMBIGUITY IS THE ANSWER

There was a heavy breath on the other end of the call, followed by a resigned, "I'll get back with you."

It wasn't until an hour before Burton was due to give his testimony that he was finally cleared to speak openly. He had done his homework and used it to build momentum at every stage of his battle with the massive bureaucracy. He brought the details to bear one last time. He laid out in the clearest terms his key findings, as well as some of the dirty games higher ups had played.

At the end of the hearings, Congress excoriated the leaders who put their own careers ahead of the safety of soldiers, and demanded that accurate tests be conducted on the Bradley, in line with Burton's plans. Somehow, he had done the impossible. With Boyd in his ear, he fought the building and won.

For all of his intense study and all of his successes, Boyd wrote almost nothing about what he discovered about competitive environments. Instead, he put his insights into an in-person briefing, called *Patterns of Conflict*, that lasted three days. Boyd revised it frequently yet refused to shorten it for anyone, no matter how high someone's rank or how great their sense of importance. This boundary had almost no effect on attendance. Nearly everyone who had the opportunity to hear Boyd's briefing cleared their schedule to be present for every second of it.

Patterns was a masterwork, the result of a rigorous and creative mind studying for years in a manner unlike anyone in the world.

Boyd began the briefing by setting the stage for everything he would discuss. Part one set out the conceptual framework and historical context, but the second part was where the talk really began. It was there that he laid out his most important revelations about what matters most when the odds are against us.

The first word out of his mouth: "Ambiguity."

HARNESS HIDDEN TRANSCRIPTS
Ambiguity as Accuracy

> Our favorite people and our favorite stories become so not by any inherent virtue, but because they illustrate something deep in the grain, something unadmitted.
>
> — JOAN DIDION

In lectures to crowds of young women, Virginia Woolf used to take her listeners through a short thought experiment. Take a moment, she said, to imagine an ornate building so large it holds every book and play and poem people have produced for thousands of years. The greats. The niche. The mediocre. This library would house everything. Row after row, on shelf on top of shelf, would sit the story of who we are, our collective public record.

After marveling at the grandeur of the architecture and the immensity of our story, Woolf would tell her listeners to imagine walking among the rows. Take in the titles, she said. Pull selections off the shelves and consume them. Pay attention to how they speak about the things you know, your lived

HARNESS HIDDEN TRANSCRIPTS

experiences and innermost feelings. Which parts are included? Which ones are absent?

Woolf's particular interest was in exploring the depictions of women throughout centuries of content, where she saw no subtlety or nuance, no depth. It wasn't that the depictions were all negative, just that they were painfully off. Where there should have been truth, there was only caricature. There were women so beautiful they inspired obsession, as well as those who were purely evil and those meant only for the background.

One could pick title after title off the shelves and feel no connection to, or visibility in, the women they contained. All those works, across all those years, added up to very little. The friendships, dreams, and intelligence of women's real lives were nowhere to be found. Woolf called this absence in the face of such abundance "the accumulation of unrecorded life."

Faulty representations are laid into the public record every day as though they are an accurate depiction of our world. They pile up and build off of each other, legitimizing and codifying a flawed whole. What Woolf realized was that more content about women, if it was made in the vein of what came before, wouldn't necessarily produce a more accurate picture of women's lives. It would only further entrench a distorted view.

Another way to think about this is to recognize what a faulty and incomplete picture the public record provides. The public record lags people's truths. It misses all that is known but not voiced openly or recorded officially. Instead of being accurate and all-encompassing, the public record is perpetually outdated

AMBIGUITY IS THE ANSWER

and off, functioning like a funhouse mirror attempting to twist reality into false forms.

The glut of content created not only today, but also throughout history, can make it easy to forget how much still goes unsaid. An abundance of wisdom is with us every day that never shows up in the public record. It is shared in trusted spaces, whispered when no one is looking, and acknowledged in subtle gestures and untraceable references by knowing parties.

This unsearchable and off-the-record knowledge was referred to by the political scientist James C. Scott as the "hidden transcripts." At their core, the hidden transcripts are a reminder that we don't document everything we know, and that not everyone is sharing everything. There are whole libraries of wisdom, insights, and observations that cannot be easily located but are as present and real as anything. And, often, while the public record says one thing, the hidden transcripts tell a very different story.

It can be dangerous to speak what is unspoken. So the hidden transcripts keep us safe while keeping undercurrents of knowledge alive. They keep us from drifting into dominant storylines and allow us to hold what we know in the face of what we're told. In the same way that Woolf illuminated flaws in the stories of women, we can recognize when the public record is off and trust in the value of what we know in the hidden transcripts.

The challenge rests in the tension of holding two types of awareness simultaneously: the world as we are told it is, and

HARNESS HIDDEN TRANSCRIPTS

the world as we know it to be. This ability to maintain two readings of the world at the same time was referred to by Homi Bhabha as "a peculiar visceral intelligence." That's because not everyone does it well. Many people are challenged by the idea that the same symbols, institutions, or interactions we experience can possess wildly oppositional meanings. And they have difficulty leaving the door open to more than a single, certain assessment, even if it means being wrong or missing out on valuable information.

So, paradoxically, a singular interpretation can be its own form of ignorance, while an ambiguous reading can be its own form of accuracy. Seeing multiple interpretations can mean seeing the world clearly. But it requires a willingness to look beyond easy or obvious readings to see what hard, hidden truths might be present as well.

Major changes often start with people observing fundamental flaws in the approaches of the day. But that doesn't mean these observations are immediately put into the public record. People don't share every insight as soon as they have it, which shouldn't come as a surprise. Significant critiques are often forced to simmer quietly until the time is right to voice them. Years before they make their bold entrances in public, they are shared with trusted parties out of sight.

Have you ever noticed…
I'm starting to think…
Is it possible that…

AMBIGUITY IS THE ANSWER

The challenge of holding onto multiple readings of symbols and circumstances comes from maintaining this awareness while the public record continues filling up with stories at odds with one's own understanding. It can be hard to hold onto what you know in the face of such forces. Woolf understood this, which is why she not only brought awareness to the gendered flaws of the public record, but also promoted the means for women to produce more honest stories and resist the fabricated ones they heard so often.

In this way, rather than allowing dominant storylines to pacify our thinking, they should be used to prompt action. As the psychiatrist and political philosopher Frantz Fanon put it, they should "serve not only as inhibitors but also as stimulants." They should serve as reminders to "get ready to do the right thing," he said.

Born on the Caribbean island of Martinique, and deeply engaged in Algeria's liberation from France, Fanon spent much of his life experiencing, understanding, and resisting colonialism. His writing on the subject was both forceful and nuanced, bringing to life the complex, twisted psychological effects of living in a world that is defined by others.

For Fanon, growing up under colonialism meant being surrounded, at all times, by signs meant to destroy his dignity. Subtle and overt symbols of domination reigned. From the flags flying atop buildings to the vicious power dynamic piercing social interactions, the drum of a dictated life never stopped beating. One was never not reminded of the way things were.

HARNESS HIDDEN TRANSCRIPTS

Publicly, these symbols of domination were depicted in positive terms. Colonial militaries were called "liberators." Their countries were beacons of "liberty" and "freedom" and "equality." Rather than domination, they were bringing "culture" and "opportunity." Anything associated with them was presented in only the most positive light publicly.

Perhaps, for the colonizers, this may have seemed like the only way to view the situation, and they may have been quite certain in their read. After all, this was the story they told themselves and the one they were invested so heavily in telling others. But for those whose land had been invaded and lives had been subjugated, the idea that a colonizing country's flag was a beacon of freedom was a sick joke. It was, in fact, the opposite: a symbol of restriction and domination. The antithesis of freedom.

Reinforced so many times and in so many ways, the dominant storyline was a reminder of the fact that, as Toni Morrison said, "definitions belonged to the definers—not the defined." And so, Fanon said, one had to live in that tension between what was said and what one knew. Despite any display of niceties, the power dynamic on colonized lands was so strong that critiques couldn't be spoken or put into the record without violent repercussions. This didn't mean the critiques went away. They didn't disappear simply because it was dangerous to voice them. Rather, they took on different forms.

It may be tempting to question the importance of realizations that lie below the surface. After all, how meaningful can

AMBIGUITY IS THE ANSWER

an insight be if it isn't shared openly? What good is knowledge that doesn't pierce the public record? But hidden transcripts are not only the preservation of intelligence. They are also preparation for its application.

Fanon's impact on the world gives good reason to reconsider any skepticism. Despite dying when only thirty-six years old, his work provided validation for the experiences of millions of people living through and resisting colonialism by putting voice to what they knew but couldn't say. By detailing the horrors and effects of living under colonialism, Fanon made the invisible palpable. He also served as one of the strongest and most direct influences on some of the world's largest political movements, especially in the latter half of the twentieth century when a host of nations fought for, and gained, independence from colonial governments.

Hidden transcripts pervade our world. Not only do we use them to point our lives in new directions, but they allow us to connect in intimate ways, to stay safe, and to navigate complex situations. They allow us to embed meaning and messages where those who need to catch them will.

The secret is to take them seriously. Find them. Listen to them. Keep close to them and pay attention to what they reveal. Notice what is evident but unacknowledged.

Rather than chasing what others say is important or always trying to find new insights, sometimes we just need to bring to life what we already know. We can break those quiet truths

HARNESS HIDDEN TRANSCRIPTS

into the open, for us and anyone else who's had to keep such a visceral awareness buried.

We can ask ourselves: What do we know but never talk about? What have we experienced but never had accurately reflected back to us? What do we see that sits in the blind spots of others?

It is there, in those answers, that we'll find what we need. It is from there that our impact will grow. Because the ideas that transform the world almost never arise suddenly, even when it feels that way. Instead, they are only the elevation of perspectives long held but just now publicized. Revolutionary ideas are often little more than hidden transcripts moved into the light.

NEVER UNDERESTIMATE FLUIDITY
Ambiguity as Opening

All greatness is improbable.

— LAO TZU

About 150 years ago, industrial manufacturing picked up significantly and ushered in a host of changes, one of which was that people started building ships out of steel instead of wood like they had been. It was a promising shift. The wooden ships had proven their effectiveness over time but had also come up against their limits. They could only be so big, go so fast, and carry so much weight. By virtue of steel's strength, the new structures were expected to expand the limits and open up new possibilities. Instead, they broke apart and sank.

There is the infamous story of the "unsinkable" *Titanic* going under after hitting an iceberg in the Atlantic Ocean, but the problem with the steel ships was actually more perni-

NEVER UNDERESTIMATE FLUIDITY

cious. They were breaking apart and sinking in fairly ordinary weather conditions, when everything should have been just fine. For some reason, the same pressures the wooden ships could handle were proving to be too much for the steel ones, with dire consequences.

The shipbuilders' bias was to mistake the strength of the structure for the strength of the materials. They assumed that because steel was strong, steel ships would be too. And for years they struggled to understand why that might not necessarily be true. After all, the problem was not some inherent weakness in the material; it was in how the ships were put together. The shipbuilders were so enamored by the material's strength that they overlooked the weak points in their plans. They failed to see that while the whole can be more than the sum of its parts, it can also be a whole lot less.

It is tempting to see the shipbuilders' bias as a historical one, the sort of flaw people make before they get the math right. But, in fact, this is the kind of mental trap we can fall into at any time, often without even realizing it.

We see strong parts and expect a strong whole. We expect a team full of star players to win. We think a creative project built with new technologies will produce a better experience. We trust great schools on a resume will make a great employee.

While these might be decent indicators of outcomes, they are far from any guarantee of success. Think about how many great teams have fallen apart because the star players couldn't get along. How many creative projects are

AMBIGUITY IS THE ANSWER

built with fancy tools but are bland in execution? How many employees look amazing on paper yet disappoint in practice? The lists are long.

Strong parts don't always make a strong whole. We can make bad soup with good ingredients. The same bricks can make a building stand for two hundred years or fall in five. It's how we assemble what we have that really matters. If we fail to put our pieces together well, we'll be no different than the early steel shipbuilders who watched their brilliant vessels sink to the bottom of the sea. We'll just be applying their bias to our problems.

This tendency to focus attention on the strongest parts of our work can be a hard one to shake. That's because, deep down, we know the things we want will not be easy. In order to push through the difficulties, we're often willing—perhaps even eager—to keep our eyes on the good parts of what we're building.

The upside of this positivity is that it can give us the drive to push ourselves to new heights. The downside is that we can forget how others see us. We can forget that while we're busy looking at our strengths, others might be looking at our weaknesses.

This was the case at the end of the twentieth century when climate researchers were shocked by the way their work was suddenly attacked. Decades of research from many of the world's smartest minds in fields ranging from oceanography to migration culminated in a single, dire conclusion that humans were significantly disrupting Earth's ecology and

NEVER UNDERESTIMATE FLUIDITY

ushering in climate changes that would profoundly affect the health and long-term viability of human life, not to mention other species' as well.

By the 1990s, the evidence for all of this was so overwhelming that the usually passive academic world began to step tentatively into public advocacy. Researchers were so concerned by what they were finding that they felt compelled to raise the alarm, to bring their conclusions to the people in hopes of creating change.

On the whole, their approach was effective. As the research moved from staid academic journals to newspapers, magazines, and television, the message was taking hold. People believed the science. They were worried about the implications. And they wanted to know what could be done, both individually and with policy.

Then something changed. It started slow, with a cadre of men showing up on television questioning whether the planet was even getting warmer. Of all the science behind climate change, measuring temperature changes was perhaps the easiest to track and understand. However, that wasn't the point. By challenging even the most obvious evidence, these new talking heads were subtly and repeatedly introducing doubt into the public conversation.

"The industry had realized that you could create the impression of controversy simply by asking questions, even if you actually knew the answers and they didn't help your case," wrote Naomi Oreskes and Erik Conway.

AMBIGUITY IS THE ANSWER

From temperature changes, the industry-backed opposition kept going. They created false equivalencies between research funded by oil companies and that funded by international scientific bodies. They claimed climate change was a total hoax. Then they admitted it was happening but argued that humans had no role in the matter. In essence, a manufactured movement was created to try everything imaginable to sway public opinion away from addressing climate change. They attacked from every angle imaginable, and often worked in flagrant contradiction of their own arguments.

To the climate researchers, who had spelled out how much damage had already been done, and where the mad-grab for profit and convenience was taking us, the counterarguments were inane. The evidence was so overwhelming it was daunting. What was the point in arguing against it? Why was there any "debate" at all? More importantly, why were the climate researchers losing it?

It's natural to feel as though we won't find ourselves in these sorts of difficult moments, that something about us and our work will keep us safe from the firebrands. The climate researchers clearly did. They were sure the quality of their work and the moral imperative of their message would protect them from attacks. But they were wrong.

Let's not kid ourselves. There are plenty of circumstances where others do not see us as we see ourselves. They don't necessarily give us the benefit of the doubt or an understanding

NEVER UNDERESTIMATE FLUIDITY

pass. They don't particularly care if what we've built is from strong materials or for good reason. Like the ocean, they will move like water and find holes in our plans.

The phenomena of unfounded attacks is far from being confined to the world of climate change. Like death and taxes, attacks on us and our work are guaranteed in this life. The trick is to learn to see ourselves through the eyes of others. To look where they would look and think how they would think. We must ask ourselves, what weak points would someone else see? Which aspects, were they to be seen and exploited, would sink our ship?

In this sense, it can be helpful to see the pieces of our lives as having two parts: their *structure* and their *story*. The story of the *Titanic* was that it was unsinkable. Its structure was shown to be otherwise. And this can be true for many situations. Competitors can seem unstoppable. Social, economic, and political systems can seem impossible to change. Underneath every story is a structure that may or may not reflect its narrative. Some structures we face are stronger in perception than in practice.

This is why it can be so problematic to adopt the framing others put on our situations. Convinced of how to see, we can be convinced of how to move. We can start to believe that what others have built is better or stronger than it is. Story and spectacle can transform our clear-eyed awareness into starry-eyed awe.

AMBIGUITY IS THE ANSWER

This is an age-old phenomenon. For centuries, myths and folktales around the world have spoken to the importance of maintaining an honest perception of the world, especially when we're being dazzled. In the "One Last Shower of Petals" story from Japan, a crowd was wowed by flowers falling off a tree. Just one man remained skeptical and, waiting out the performance, revealed it to be a hoax. The "Gold, Gold" story from China teaches a similar lesson, as do a number of Aesop's fables.

One of Nelson Mandela's favorite folktales was the East African story of an enormous bird that came to do harm to a village. Waves of adults were sent to fend it off but, as they got closer, the adults all became enchanted by the bird's song and gave up. Only after a group of children pursued the bird, and resisted being swayed by its sounds, was the village finally protected.

A captivating song. A shower of petals. A pile of gold. The details vary but the lesson is the same: *actions follow perceptions*.

Since grand gestures and even more mundane means can frame how we see, without realizing it, they can lead us away from finding the openings we need to break new futures free. Suddenly, the only tactics that seem "right" and "acceptable" for us to take are the ones that are also ineffective and predictable. If we aren't careful, we can end up following the protocol of the palace, as if its whole purpose isn't to protect the palace.

While structures are designed to resist the forces placed against them, they are not monoliths. They aren't uniformly strong everywhere. Instead, their designs are the result of any

NEVER UNDERESTIMATE FLUIDITY

number of trade-offs, and in those trade-offs sit openings. Finding them can be a difficult and improbable task, with many ways to fail and a very small number of ways to succeed.

This is why a fluid, ambiguous approach can be so helpful. There are times when we miss our openings not because they don't exist, but because we aren't moving in ways that allow us to find them. A fluid ambiguity is a faith in uncovering, a belief in possibility existing beyond what's apparent or probable. It enables us to look at the structures we're told are impenetrable and believe that our actions, once initiated, will uncover the openings necessary for making our impact. What we need will emerge from the way we move.

Back in the 1770s, Peruvians were facing down the seemingly impenetrable structure of Spanish colonialism and trying to find a new way forward. The vicious colonial structure had been in place for more than 200 years and it seemed to be getting stronger all the time. Ever unsatiated, the colonizers continued implementing more and more forms of extraction and exploitation.

"Spanish America had become in those times the theater of the most extensive tyranny, but the yoke lay most heavily on the necks of Peruvian Indians," explained Gregorio Funes.

One of the most hated practices was a brutal labor draft, called the *mita*, which forced indigenous Peruvians to leave their communities, travel 600 miles at their own expense, and work in the hot and dangerous Potosí silver mines. The Potosí silver was so plentiful and valuable that it "powered the engine of the empire." It made Spain one of the richest nations in the world, but its extraction was the stuff of nightmares.

There was pain in other areas of life as well. Indigenous Peruvians were locked inside textile mills and forced to work. They were required to buy goods from powerful merchants at inflated prices. And, on top of these forms of domination, the colonizers decided to build out an ever more aggressive tax system, expanding the number of items taxed and drastically increasing the rates. Between 1772 and 1776, the Spanish tripled the sales tax. Between 1750 and 1820, the amount of money collected in Cuzco through the Indian head tax, a tax on each indigenous Peruvian simply for being who they were, increased by a factor of sixteen.

As a result of these actions, both the colonial story and structure grew stronger. The Spanish were doing anything they wanted and it looked like they would continue being able to. But, as the historian Charles Walker explained, "The Spanish had initially believed that Indians were too cowardly and mestizos too 'unfortunate' (*desdichada suerte*) to lead an uprising; they would soon learn they were wrong."

That happened in November 1780. It was then that Tupac Amaru and his wife, the logistically minded Micaela Bastidas, had what they needed. Less a collection of tangible resources than a set of knowledge, experiences, and relationships, the couple realized that the widespread frustration with colonial rule had shifted into a new willingness to act.

NEVER UNDERESTIMATE FLUIDITY

Walker explained that Amaru, "had the respect of Cuzco's Indians, reasons to loathe the Spanish, and the experience and worldliness to organize an uprising."

By the end of the month, he would launch the largest uprising ever in the Americas. And it wasn't just the willingness to start that was so impactful; it was the way the rebels moved fluidly, uncovering openings in the colonial structure, and finding places where they had advantages. Rather than concentrating their forces in one place, they would unite and disperse in an instant, somehow managing to be here, there, and nowhere simultaneously, operating as a sort of intangible omnipresence.

This fluid ambiguity made the movements of the Tupac Amaru Rebellion hard to grasp and even harder to anticipate. Like the ocean, the rebels were able to put pressure on many places at once, see what worked, and keep going. Once the first cracks in the colonial structure were exposed, other openings were revealed as well.

For instance, because the Spanish believed so strongly that the rebels were incapable of launching and leading such a major effort, they started turning in on themselves, accusing one another of betrayal and ousting each other. In this way, fluidity not only found existing openings, it created new ones, producing a chain reaction of possibilities.

Despite the tyranny of the Spanish colonizers, when all the harm they caused led to a rebellion of such major scale

AMBIGUITY IS THE ANSWER

and significance, they were still surprised. After all, like the shipbuilders, they had been taken in by the story about the strength of what they built.

And when, in the years that followed the rebellion, the Spanish attempted to make sense of what happened by retracing Tupac Amaru's steps, they were stunned by all he had accomplished, by all the openings that he and his wife and the rebels were able to find by moving fluidly against the structure that was believed to have been so strong for so long.

THE APPEAL OF NOT KNOWING

Ambiguity as Attraction

If you can't be free, be a mystery.

— RITA DOVE

Though Harlem has always been New York's undisputed home of jazz, like other royal figures of the art form, Billie Holiday eventually moved to Queens. She was joined there by friends who had performed more times than anyone could count and were, collectively, still innovating, recording, and touring.

Life in Queens was a respite from the long drives and late nights, from the unscrupulous club owners and the never-ending demands of managers and industry folks. Queens was where the backyards were big enough for the neighborhood to gather for barbecue, where cultural icons converted their hard work into homes where their families could spread out. In other words, with watchful eyes elsewhere, Queens allowed jazz greats to just *be*.

AMBIGUITY IS THE ANSWER

Holiday's time in the borough overlapped with that of the great trumpeter Miles Davis. In music, the two of them were larger-than-life figures, both known for constant experimentation and utter originality. In Queens, though, their days were a bit more traditional.

On Saturday afternoons, Davis would ride a borrowed bicycle through the streets over to Holiday's house. She'd be waiting for him, as well as his two year old son, who often accompanied Davis on the visits. At her place, they'd play and talk for hours. And then, the next Saturday, they'd do it all over again.

Holiday was a hardworking musical genius who transformed singing and influenced at least a century of great vocalists. She was a bisexual Black woman who embodied new notions of freedom and had relationships with people across race and class lines. She rose from poverty and childhood trauma to magazine covers and sold out shows at Carnegie Hall. And she did all of this in the face of Jim Crow, under relentless governmental pressure, and within an industry calibrated to take advantage of its artists.

Yet her enigmatic life was made not only in the headlines but also in simpler times like those in Queens, watching Miles Davis come and go on a bicycle. These "amplified moments of withholding, escape and possibility," as Saidiya Hartman has called them, hint at a more complete picture of who she was but never fully fill in the details. Like anyone with real style, there's something intangible about Holiday. She captivated

THE APPEAL OF NOT KNOWING

even as she confused, intrigued even as she evaded. Her life contradicted and defied a singular narrative. And this ability to somehow be both at hand and out of reach only added to her lasting appeal.

After years of singing in clubs and joints of all kinds, often at more than one place in a night, Holiday got a break when the owner of Harlem's famed Apollo Theater was invited to hear her sing. Before attending the performance, the owner wanted to know what he was getting into. What could he expect? What kind of singing style did Holiday have?

The answer he received was undefined yet adamant: "I don't know what it is but you got to hear her."

Some people might be offended that they couldn't be summed up or described more easily, but Holiday was pleased when she heard the story. Like Duke Ellington, who believed the highest praise one could receive was to be considered "beyond category," Holiday appreciated existing beyond easy categorization. "This, I always figured, was the biggest compliment they could pay me," she said.

After all, jazz is rooted in the blues and, as Ralph Ellison reminded us, "The blues is an art of ambiguity." Songs can do many things at once, with even seemingly straightforward lyrics carrying multiple important meanings. For instance, a song about longing for being treated right could be about love from a partner or, just as easily, about demanding justice from a nation. The ambiguous nature and presentation allows them

AMBIGUITY IS THE ANSWER

to do and be about both simultaneously. Those who are meant to pick up on the multiple messages tend to have no problem finding them.

The art of ambiguity is a reminder that there have always been, and always will be, ways of conveying everything while divulging nothing. Rooted in and carrying forward a Black radical aesthetic, the blues tradition of ambiguity possesses what the philosopher Fred Moten has called the "dual possibility" of saying so much and so little at the same time. Holiday emerged from and built upon this tradition.

"She was able to set in profound motion deeply disturbing disjunctions between overt statements and their aesthetic meanings," explained Angela Davis.

In our era of short attention spans and content overload, it can feel as though there's little patience for work that requires extra effort to be understood. But in practice this isn't necessarily true. Ambiguity can stop people in their tracks. It draws them in with something that can't be quickly processed or categorized. It is counterintuitive, but people's interest often increases along with their confusion. Or, as Ellison said, the search for understanding "often baffles when it most intrigues."

There's an appeal in not knowing. While we might long for certainty, it is often the people and things we struggle to fully make sense of that attract our attention. *What am I hearing? What am I looking at? What does this mean?* This search to unpack what we're experiencing casts a spell over us. We keep listening. We keep looking. We keep longing.

THE APPEAL OF NOT KNOWING

Ambiguity demands attention. Our brains want to figure things out, so it is refreshing to come across experiences that can't be quickly processed like everything else. By asking more of us, by resisting the urge to regress to the mean, ambiguity opens us up to experiences we didn't realize we were missing and never could've communicated our need for. As confusing as it can be for a time, the reason we love ambiguity is because it gives us something we can't get anywhere else.

In 2012, the comedian Tig Notaro gave an audience exactly that type of experience. She was performing at a club in Los Angeles called Largo. "It's probably going to be a mess," she admitted, while waiting to go on stage. In her hands were crumpled up notes with untested jokes scribbled on them.

One of the central traits of stand-up comedians is a willingness to not know how something will go. They step on stage and try out untested material all the time, hoping for the best. Notaro had been through that trial-and-error process plenty of times over the years. Tonight was different, though. Yes, the jokes were untested. But she also had a secret to share.

The evening's host gave her a touching introduction while she stood in the wings. Then she walked out from behind a tall red curtain, into the lights, and up to the microphone at the center of the stage. She started speaking while the crowd was still cheering.

Hello, good evening.
Hello.
I have cancer.

AMBIGUITY IS THE ANSWER

Those last three words seemed to mix with the others as though they were an afterthought, spoken with the same generic energy that starts so many standup sets.

I have cancer, how are you? Hi, how are you? Is everybody having a good time? I have cancer, how are you?

The audience seemed unaware of the news woven in between the bland opening lines. They caught on soon enough.

Tig Notaro had cancer.

Barely more than a week had passed from the time Notaro learned she was diagnosed with cancer in both of her breasts to the moment she walked onto that stage. One of the reasons she went ahead with the show at all, in the midst of such scary news, was because she thought it might be her last chance to ever perform. The doctors believed the cancer might have already spread to her lymph nodes.

Notaro let the weight of the news settle into the room. Then she went on to explain that her diagnosis actually came on the heels of a series of painful experiences. First, her health had suddenly deteriorated, and she was hospitalized for over a week with a potentially life-threatening infection called *C. difficile.* Just days after being released from the hospital, and still very weak, Notaro learned that in a sudden freak accident, her mother tripped, hit her head, and was in a coma. A day later, her mother passed away. Shortly after the funeral, Notaro's girlfriend broke up with her. And then she got diagnosed with cancer. All of this occurred in a span of only about four months.

THE APPEAL OF NOT KNOWING

Comedians tend to think few topics are entirely off-limits, so cancer and death are not forbidden from being discussed. But to *have* cancer and talk about it and make jokes about it when the diagnosis is still visibly, audibly fresh was something else entirely. Notaro went on stage and processed her heart-breaking news in real time, as raw and poised as anyone could be in such a moment.

"It's going to be okay," Notaro said at one point. She was consoling an audience member having a particularly tough time processing the news. "Well, I don't know about with me," she added, "but you're going to be okay."

The set was full of these kinds of moments. Laughter at the wrong times. Sadness when it would've been okay to laugh. No one knew exactly what to do or how to act. The whole situation was too heartbreaking to be purely funny. Yet it was also too challenging to not take solace in Notaro's willingness to somehow find and share so many moments of humor.

Luckily, we don't need to know what a moment means in order to cherish it. While the audience may have shown up expecting comedy, what they got instead was much more mean-ingful. In the span of a lunch break, Notaro created an experience so moving and complicated as to defy categorization.

In the months after her set, the audio from that night at Largo was released to the public, under the ambiguous-looking title *Live*. It sold more than 100,000 copies in six weeks and went on to be nominated for a Grammy award.

AMBIGUITY IS THE ANSWER

"It's a startling release," wrote *The Guardian*, "one that redefines the boundaries of what comedy can achieve."

Rolling Stone was even more direct, calling *Live* "an amazing, uncomfortable document."

Even the promotional material accompanying the release avoided the usual comedy lauds and, instead, spoke to the appeal of its ambiguous nature: "I can't really describe it but I was crying and laughing and listening like never in my life."

Notaro described the evening as "something I don't think any of us had really ever experienced."

I don't know what it is but you have to hear her.

There is a rare power in one's ability to not be reduced. Notaro and Holiday both managed to create works that exist beyond easy interpretation, that are ambiguous and indescribable, yes, but also captivating and unforgettable as well.

Even today, more than six decades since her passing, Holiday maintains this hold over people. Everything about this extraordinary woman, from her entrancing voice to how she navigated issues beyond her control, remains wrapped in an aura of mystery. She is, in some ways, still unknowable. There seems to always be a detail that counters the popular narrative, always something that calls into question the quest for certainty. Her history is not vague or empty. Instead, we are pulled in different directions simultaneously, swimming in an intriguing flotsam of inspiration, frustration, and yearning.

"The more we claim to pull back layers, the more we expose contradictions and complexity," explained Farah Jasmine Griffin.

THE APPEAL OF NOT KNOWING

As a result, Griffin adds, Holiday "never goes where we expect her to go."

At times, it can feel like a cottage industry dedicated to making sense of Holiday has cropped up since her passing. But this is really only a continuation of what she experienced during her life. Because, in the midst of the limited stories we have, a clear but subtle pattern emerges. Over and over, we see people struggling to grasp what she went through. In pursuit of a single way to reduce her, the fact that she might have been a complex character at a complex time seems to be too much for many to accept. They seem shocked that she could hold so many dichotomies, as though glamor negates strength or struggle is any kind of mark against greatness.

Holiday had been sticking up for herself for years, as a kid in clubs with adults, on tours as the only woman, on the frontlines of racism, and against threats from her own government. When she was thrust into another crisis and those around her could not fathom that what was happening to her could really be happening, Holiday didn't give them soliloquies or hand out history lessons. She didn't connect all of the dots or spell everything out for them. Instead, with a look and the sparest of sounds, she let them know that if they were shocked this one thing could happen, then they were nowhere near ready for the whole picture.

Over and over, in these kinds of moments, we see that others were stunned by what was happenings and she was not. Holiday had been here, been through this kind of thing, before.

AMBIGUITY IS THE ANSWER

She knew exactly what she was up against. She had seen it and known it and lived it every day of her life.

In early 1959, Holiday flew to London for what turned out to be her last television appearance. In addition to "Porgy" and a haunting version of "Strange Fruit," she sang one of her classics: "Please Don't Talk About Me When I'm Gone."

The thing about ambiguity is that it keeps people talking. It keeps us chasing an answer we may never find. Even as we dig deeper and draw in others for help, we can feel certainty slip further away. And yet, in the pursuit, our appreciation and awe only grow larger. The appeal of not knowing persists.

INTRODUCE ALTERNATIVES

Ambiguity as Intrigue

Everything you see ain't really how it be.

— YASIIN BEY

At a certain point, the narratives we were raised on break down and the world finds a way to give us the knowledge we need. There's no telling how or when we learn these lessons but, when we do, it's important to listen to them, since they might just ask us to remap our sense of the world.

As the sculptor and painter Anne Truitt put it, "Forced into certain circumstances, we are forced to learn what those circumstances teach us."

For her, it was a deep appreciation for the ability to endure that guided much of her life. Truitt wasn't sure where this willful devotion to see things through came from. Maybe she picked it up from her mother's temperament? Perhaps it was developed over the course of her many long, grueling days in the studio?

AMBIGUITY IS THE ANSWER

Either way, Truitt felt strongly that there was something enjoyable about getting through an especially difficult project, and something special about possessing the kind of stubbornness it takes to endure hard times. "It can be, quite literally, the only way to survive," she said.

In her forties, after years of the "familiar brunt" of grinding through her circumstances, Truitt had a simple but meaningful revelation. Having prided herself on endurance for so much of her life, she realized that she didn't need to just get through difficult moments, she could *alter* them. Like her art, her life could bear her imprint. Recapping the moment of insight in her journal, she wrote, "it occurred to me that I could use the energy I had been putting into endurance to *change* my life."

There's no denying that a stubborn willingness to persist through hard times is a prerequisite for much in this life. What Truitt came to realize, however, is that our issue might not be that we're no good at enduring through tough times, but that we're actually *too good* at it. Many of us endure by default. We put up with, and get through, situations that aren't glamorous or easy all the time. Enduring isn't some impossibility. We know it. We do it. And in fact, like Truitt, our ability to endure is an area about which many of us feel a deep sense of pride. It feels good to know we can if we need to.

In a time where demands pile up on us from every direction, our ability to carry so many responsibilities while balancing our needs with those of others is nothing short of impressive. Get-

INTRODUCE ALTERNATIVES

ting through it all *is* worth celebrating. But Truitt's revelation is an important one to consider: We shouldn't be so proud of our ability to endure that we fail to fix what holds us back. If we're going to be called upon to use our energy, let's not waste it just getting through situations that could've been avoided. Let's use it to change our circumstances.

The question then is how? Once we realize circumstances are more pliable than they appear, how do we, in fact, ply them?

The natural world provides a simple but useful example. Throughout Africa, birds in the *Anthoscopus* genus build beautiful hanging nests that look like soft, fuzzy balloons. But the truly genius part is in their architecture. The birds build their nests with two entrances and two rooms. One entrance is small and unassuming. It's hidden under a small flap that can be sealed from the inside and leads to the part of the nest where the birds live. The other entrance is wide and obvious but leads to an empty room, known as a false chamber.

Instead of enduring predators entering their nests, the birds put extra time, energy, and materials into building an entrance and a room they never intend to use. They make it easy for snakes to go to the wrong place, and it works often enough that the birds keep doing it.

We can think of this as creating ambiguity through the introduction of alternatives. It's an approach that belies the popular focus on efficiencies and optimizations. Ambiguity sends us out past the language of operations. It takes us to

AMBIGUITY IS THE ANSWER

where cause and effect are only loosely, optimistically coupled, asking us to spend time and energy on activities that are not immediately or even assuredly valuable.

Ambiguity's effectiveness stems from the ability of alternatives to catch the eye and demand consideration. Done right, the pump fake and feint look too good to ignore. They are begging to be weighed as real possibilities. Instead of being extra work, alternatives assist by pointing attention elsewhere. They create the space we need to move.

This isn't a tactical consideration; it's a strategic one. Because in every effort to change circumstances there is a catch-22: the need to promote plans and the need to protect them. Big announcements, which feel good in the moment, risk divulging too much. Keeping plans to ourselves can feel safe but stunt our progress. So hard work and good intentions eventually reach a point where strategy becomes necessary as well. We must be thoughtful about what we're doing and how it's revealed. Everyone doesn't get to know everything.

Kobe Bryant was coming to this realization when he was just seventeen years old, as he prepared to enter the 1996 NBA draft. Despite his young age and the fact he was coming straight out of high school, he was seen as one of the best players in that year's class.

While it's tempting to see sports as a purely athletic endeavor, at the end of the day, each team is fundamentally a business. By the time draft day rolls around, financial interests have taken hold and, ironically, the athletes get caught in the current.

INTRODUCE ALTERNATIVES

Great players get picked by bad teams all the time and there's almost nothing they can do about it. The teams hold almost all of the power.

The situation was no different for Bryant. All signs pointed to him being selected by the Nets, who were based in New Jersey at the time. The team's head coach saw Bryant as a once-in-a-generation player who possessed a rare combination of talent and competitiveness that could dominate on the court. This young star could be the centerpiece around which the whole franchise was built.

The team's love for Bryant wasn't reciprocated, however, and it made for a bumpy path to draft day. For months in the lead up, Bryant's camp pushed a whisper campaign saying *Buyer beware!* Bryant was so against playing in New Jersey, the rumor went, that he was planning to move to Italy and play basketball oversees instead if they picked him. The Nets would embarrass themselves and waste a first round draft pick for nothing.

By the time draft day came around, there was no way to tell what was true or would really happen. The straightforward decision based on Bryant's skill became muddied by the possibility he would leave for Italy. The team had to contend with a new set of questions. Was anyone straight out of high school worth such a risk? Who would take the blame if the decision went south? The introduction of a compelling alternative created an unavoidable ambiguity and, in the end, it was too much.

With the eighth pick in the 1996 NBA draft, the New Jersey Nets selected...Kerry Kittles.

AMBIGUITY IS THE ANSWER

Bryant's camp was ecstatic. By adding more ingredients to the decision-making pot—in this case, a feint about leaving for Italy—they convinced the Nets to pass on Bryant even though they wanted him. Bryant's team spent extra energy promoting a path they weren't committed to in order to clear the way for their real goal.

"Most players, when they're drafted, rarely have the opportunity to have their dreams fulfilled," said Arn Tellem, Bryant's agent at the time. "But we were in a position to do it, so we went for it, and we achieved it."

Not only did the Nets not pick Bryant but, behind the scenes, a separate deal had been secretly arranged to put him on the Los Angeles Lakers, where he played every game of his career.

Over the course of twenty seasons, Bryant scored more than 33,000 points, including 81 in a single game. He won five NBA championships and was selected as an All-Star eighteen times. Of course, none of this would have been possible without his unrivaled work ethic and competitive spirit. But we have to wonder, too, how his career would have turned out had he thrown up his hands during the draft and endured two decades with the Nets.

It can be odd to think that there's a usefulness in putting time and energy into paths we never intend to take, especially when these sorts of approaches are rarely put on the table or included in the stories we tell about how people succeed. Cutting out the role of ambiguity from our histories handcuffs our potential in the future. It holds us back by hiding

INTRODUCE ALTERNATIVES

knowledge we need. Because there comes a time when we must acknowledge that the lofty story we tell about the power of hard work and endurance bumps up against the fact that, even in the case of someone who embodied the narrative as completely as Kobe Bryant, ambiguity ensured that one of the hardest working athletes spent his time building his career in the right place, instead of wasting it elsewhere. And, as we're about see, even in the most brutal battles of attrition, ambiguity was a constant partner creating the conditions necessary for success.

By 1943, during the Second World War, it became clear to the Allies that a major invasion was going to be necessary to stop Nazi Germany. Allied leaders decided early on that Normandy, France, would be the place they'd attempt to turn the tides of the war. What we now remember as D-Day was designed to be the largest amphibious invasion in history, with more than 150,000 people involved on the first day alone. But that was also part of the problem.

The planners had to figure out how to organize and launch such an enormous operation without tipping their hand, while their every move was being watched by the other side. This wasn't their only challenge. The planners also had to contend with the fact that Adolf Hitler was expecting an invasion *and* had the resources to stop it.

So, in addition to the plans for the invasion, a separate ambiguity-producing effort was launched, called Operation Bodyguard. The idea was to protect the truth of what was really being planned by confusing Hitler about the location and timing of the invasion. And then Bodyguard would continue to subtly convince him the Normandy invasion was only a distraction and that a much larger one was still coming elsewhere.

Like Kobe Bryant's feint about going to Italy in order to go to Los Angeles, the Allies pointed Hitler's attention to the Pas de Calais region of northern France in order to land at Normandy. To do so, they created an entire evidence base for the story they wanted to be believed. They flew conspicuous flights over the region, knowing they would be spotted. They created a fictional military group consisting of a million troops, and leaked details about it to the other side. They even brought in a large number of theater hands and movie set designers to build elaborate manufacturing scenes meant to support the story. One *ruse de guerre* after another was used to keep Hitler's mind glued to the Pas de Calais, despite all the actual evidence that an invasion was coming near Normandy.

The Allies did everything in their power to mask their true plans but, as D-Day approached, there was no way to know if Bodyguard was working. Did the Nazis see through the strategy? Were they ready for what was coming? Political leaders may have had their optimisms, but for those thousands of young adults climbing into airplanes and aboard ships, there was no way of knowing what awaited them on the other side of the English Channel.

The landings were far from perfect. Thousands of people

INTRODUCE ALTERNATIVES

lost their lives and many of the initial goals went unreached. But, crucially, they were successful enough to establish footholds that allowed more than a million additional troops to eventually land. A constellation of many seemingly minor and unrelated details came together to make it possible.

Our instinct is usually to celebrate our wins. Elated with what we've accomplished, we want to tell the world what we've done. Had the Allies wanted to do the same, in the hours and days after the initial landing, the option was available. They could have announced that the fate of the war rested on success in Normandy. They could have rattled off details about the enormous scope of the operation and how it would grow in the coming days, or explained how so much depended on this effort going well.

Instead of gloating about the early success, they downplayed its importance. Continuing the important work of Bodyguard, they hinted that other invasions in other areas would be of much greater importance. Normandy was called simply "the first of a series of landings." *This is nothing*, they seemed to be saying. *The really important stuff will happen elsewhere.*

All of this played into the belief they had cultivated in Hitler to underestimate the importance of Normandy and overestimate the role of the Pas de Calais. This was critical because if Hitler saw the Normandy invasion for what it was—a strategic success rather than simply a tactical one—he still had the means to crush it. But instead of sending significant reinforcements

AMBIGUITY IS THE ANSWER

to Normandy, Hitler kept some of his best troops in the Pas de Calais waiting for an invasion that would never come. By the time he realized what happened, his days were numbered.

After the war, soldiers made a startling discovery. Despite all the effort to keep the plans for D-Day under wraps, it turned out that, at some point, they had been leaked to the other side. Hitler had them in his possession. But, because of Bodyguard, they weren't the only ones.

The real plans were found filed alongside dozens of alternatives the Allies generated pointing to invasions at different times and places. Some of those plans contained truth, but many more of them led to false chambers. By the time D-Day occurred, Hitler was swimming in so many alternative possibilities he didn't know what deserved his attention, even when it was staring him in the face.

There was no way to pinpoint which pieces of Bodyguard mattered most but it was clear the constellation of activities succeeded. They changed the environment enough to change the outcome of the war. The production of ambiguity did something nothing else in the arsenal could.

A DISTINCTIVE CHARACTER
Ambiguity as Form

> All I want to know / for my own protection /
> is are we capable / of whatever / whenever.
>
> — ESSEX HEMPHILL

When the esteemed experimental and documentary filmmaker Marlon Riggs pictured his friend Gene, he didn't see him as a single image. Instead, Riggs saw different versions of Gene superimposed with one another, overlapping and melding together. One particularly memorable version appeared in Riggs' own groundbreaking film, *Tongues Untied*, where Riggs remembered his friend "standing upright, tuxedoed, finger-snapping, smoothly defiant."

In some ways, this Gene is larger than life and lives forever. As part of *Tongues Untied*, he's traveled the world, projected on the big screen in cities from Berkeley to Berlin. This wasn't necessarily anticipated. What the critic Wesley Morris called Riggs' "unclassifiable scrapbook of black gay male sensibility"

AMBIGUITY IS THE ANSWER

was originally supposed to be a much shorter and more conventional film, only shown to a small number of groups.

Riggs' original plan for *Tongues Untied* was to use the same powerful, if somewhat removed, style of filmmaking he had used in his earlier work. This approach had been drilled into him as the right way to create and had, in fact, recently earned him an Emmy award. Accordingly, Riggs did everything he could to stay out of the film. With a kind and an endearing sense of humor, he joked that, like a journalist, he was trying to find others to say the things he had already arrived at in his mind.

But in the same way that one version of Gene could not be pulled fully apart from the others, Riggs realized that he could not separate himself from his work. There was no way a film about being a Black gay man could ever not be personal for him. He had learned and experienced and worked through too much for it to be otherwise. His own story could not be cut out from the conversations he was facilitating.

"I had to say the things that I actually wanted other people to say," reflected Riggs.

To do so, he needed to find a form beyond what he had been trained to use, one that expanded beyond his field's conventions. It wasn't about being experimental for the sake of being experimental. Rather, he was creating a form capable of accounting for all he hoped to accomplish. So, like the superimposed images of Gene, *Tongues Untied* layered poetry, dance, humor, protests, storytelling, and more. He allowed the pieces to swirl into a new shape, and found himself fortified in the process.

A DISTINCTIVE CHARACTER

"My feeling is that there are imperatives in one's life," Riggs said. "There are some things you've got to do. You don't know all the answers. You don't know all of the consequences—but you've got to do something because you know it's right."

When the film premiered in San Francisco, Gene was in poor health. Riggs dedicated the evening to his friend's quick recovery and, thankfully, when Riggs visited him in the hospital days later, he seemed to be improving.

"So clearly you spoke, so confident you seemed," Riggs remembered.

But just two weeks later, Gene was in the intensive care unit, and Riggs was back in the hospital visiting him with friends. This time, Gene lay in his hospital bed, barely able to speak. One of the friends reached out and held his hands as a gesture to say *We are here for you*. Riggs noticed a pained look form on Gene's face.

"You're hurting him," Riggs said. "Holding his hand hurts."

Even a tender, loving touch was too much for Gene's body to handle at this point. The friend let go and Gene's face relaxed.

"Do you think I'm going to make it?" Gene asked weakly, with his eyes still closed.

The friends glanced at each other.

"They're trying a new drug," a former lover replied. "But you have to rest. You have to stop fighting the respirator. Let it breathe for you. Rest so the drug can start to work."

This was another part of the superimposed images Riggs saw: Gene in the hospital. Gene at the end.

AMBIGUITY IS THE ANSWER

The early years of HIV had a way of collapsing time, of squeezing the space not only between *healthy* and *sick*, but also the *past, present*, and *future. Gene during filming. Gene snapping on the big screen. Gene dying.* Each moment was superimposed over the others, as though they were layers of film all playing out at once.

This simultaneity was no philosophical exercise for Riggs. It was personal, as the images he saw were not only of his friend. They were also of himself. Remembering the moment in the hospital at Gene's bedside, Riggs wrote in a posthumous letter to his friend, "I studied you as I might study a mirror, witnessed the reflection of my own probable future, my not too dissimilar past."

Riggs, too, had been diagnosed with HIV and he, too, knew the medications of 1989 would not work. Like Gene, he was also embedded in and supported by a community that would create new artistic works one day and visit a friend in the hospital the next. And while many of us have been relearning the interconnected nature of things, the overlaps and intersections had long been clear to Riggs' community. There was simply no understanding an individual without understanding those around them. As Riggs affirmed in his work, "My life is of value and so is the life of my community."

The writer E.B. White once told an interviewer that the difficulty with each day was that one had to decide how to use it. "If the world were merely seductive, that would

A DISTINCTIVE CHARACTER

be easy," he said. "If it were merely challenging, that would be no problem." But instead, the world is a bit of both. So the writer who penned timeless children's tales, along with hundreds of essays on nature and the human condition, had to choose whether to focus on working to preserve the good in the world or simply enjoying it. *To save or savor?* he asked himself each morning.

There is a certain temptation in imagining, like White, that we might divvy up our days so clearly, as though loving hard or working hard could simply be assigned to this or that place on the calendar. Instead, the parts intertwine and, in the process of trying to pluck one out from another, we realize how connected they truly are. The urge to savor the last moments with a lover might come in tandem with the urge to scream in the streets until it saves their life. We might mourn and mobilize at the same time, caretake and future build in the same act. In the same breath, we might revel, rest, and resist.

This is especially important to remember in the face of difficult challenges. As politics change and cultures shift, as new crises emerge, it can be easy to feel overwhelmed. It can seem like there are too many issues at play, too many problems braided too tightly together, to not feel daunted in the face of it all. Rather than sacrifice our focus on one piece for another, it is in these times that we must find the forms, as ambiguous as they may need to be, that allow us to do and be all that is required of us.

AMBIGUITY IS THE ANSWER

It was on June 5, 1981, that the first article describing what would come to be known as HIV showed up in a Centers for Disease Control and Prevention publication. Its banal title, "Pneumocystis Pneumonia—Los Angeles," belied its devastating nature. Five young gay men between the ages of twenty-nine and thirty-six were confirmed to have a form of pneumonia that only shows up when the immune system stops protecting the body and, though early conjectures were made, there was no clear understanding of why it was happening.

A young Harvey Milk–mentored politico named Cleve Jones remembered reading the article over and over in his office. Just the day before, he had strolled through San Francisco's Dolores Park thinking about the potential of the queer community's political power. "Anything was possible," he remembered thinking.

The next morning, he went to work and came across the CDC publication in a stack of mail on his desk. After reading and rereading the article in disbelief, Jones grabbed a pair of scissors and cut it out. Before pinning the piece to a corkboard above his desk, he scrawled a note onto the page: *just when things were looking up*.

"By 1985, almost everyone I knew was dead or dying or caring for someone who was dying," said Jones.

"That's how we lived then," he added. "Our friends died; we made new friends; then they died. We found new friends yet again; then watched as they died. It went on and on and on."

A DISTINCTIVE CHARACTER

If the frontlines of HIV were a site of devastation, behind the scenes was one of dysfunction. Government agencies limped along pretending to care. Pharmaceutical companies showed little interest in getting involved. Researchers were counseled that working on anything associated with gay men was a career-ending move. Hospitals even turned people away for fear of being associated with AIDS. Just about every aspect of an effective response, from accurate testing and accessible health services to the development of effective medications, was delayed for years.

HIV/AIDS was a crisis met by indifference. While it contained a host of evergreen issues and players, like timid liberals and capitalizing conservatives, it was an altogether new amalgam. Never before had all of the pieces—politics, homophobia, business, media, and more—come together in such a dazzling display of danger.

In 1989, the same year *Tongues Untied* premiered, the *New York Times* editorial board published their take on the crisis. In a piece titled "Why Make AIDS Worse Than It Is," they wrote with heartless confidence that "Once all susceptible members are infected, the numbers of new victims will decline." It was nearly a decade into the devastation wrought by the virus and their openly stated plan was to sit by while thousands and then millions of people became infected.

"What AIDS revealed was not the problem of the virus; what AIDS revealed was the problems of our society," said the artist and activist Zoe Leonard. "It was this fissure through which everything, all the ways in which our society isn't working, became really clear."

The HIV/AIDS movement's great success was to recognize and utilize, rather than discount and ignore, the interrelated nature of the many factors. It was to see the countless issues as bound up with one another. Like the approach Riggs took in making *Tongues Untied*, the inclusion of this unique combination of factors became an opportunity to expand the picture of what a movement could look like by allowing it to move into previously untapped realms. The situation was unprecedented, so the strategies were as well.

Embroiled in crisis and surrounded by insouciance, the HIV/AIDS movement adopted what Steven Epstein called a "distinctive character." It took on a form that was both like and unlike previous movements. One might look at it and see familiar components, but there was also much more happening than anyone might expect or be familiar with.

There was loud, spectacular, in-the-street activism. And there was quiet, palliative care. There was the passage of watershed public policy. And there were underground health services. There was art and messaging that witnessed and empowered. And there was painstaking research into the problems of, and potential solutions for, the design of experimental drug trials. The movement worked in so many forums and at such an urgent pace that many queer people quickly found themselves in the position of knowing more than doctors and policy makers about

A DISTINCTIVE CHARACTER

the virus, opportunistic infections, potential medications, and the range of services needed.

The movement's ambiguous form emerged out of the urgencies of the moment and the need to usher in lasting change. Different histories and knowledge bases came together to build a new, expanded way of working. The moving parts were many and there was too much to do to only focus in one area at a time. The movement's various arms could work on issues of greatest importance to them with the understanding that all of the pieces were necessary and connected to the others.

This orientation was reflected in a strategy Sarah Schulman called *simultaneity of action*. "It was a simultaneous approach of literally designing change while escalating pressure on the society at large to step up and be accountable," she explained.

Activists often had to both call out ineffective approaches and design new solutions for institutions to implement. Part of the reason for this was that, in the early years of the movement, friend and foe were often overlapping categories. Activists didn't have the luxury of simply opposing federal agencies, pharmaceutical companies, and media outlets because of their negligent concern for people living with HIV/AIDS. What they needed was for them to move in more effective ways and with far greater urgency. So the relationships were simultaneously adversarial and collaborative. They might protest an institution one day and present new solutions to them the next.

AMBIGUITY IS THE ANSWER

It was during the filming of *Tongues Untied* that Marlon Riggs learned he was living with HIV. Almost immediately, it changed how he approached the film.

"Funny how crisis has a way of either deepening or disrupting our delusions," Riggs said.

In order for *Tongues Untied* to do everything he wanted, like the movement, he had to expand its form. He needed to move beyond his training, into a new realm. And so he let his vision broaden, fusing together formerly discrete categories to build an ambiguous form capable of embodying everything he sought to do. He spliced poetry with protest, and merged humor with tenacity, allowing the work to take on a new shape.

Not only was Riggs' expansive new form effective—*Tongues Untied* remains a landmark work that continues to inspire today—but it was also successful. The film won awards in categories ranging from best documentary to best performance art. And while Riggs might have initially intended to use more traditional methods, he ultimately allowed himself the freedom to see beyond them, to resist confining his new awareness into a familiar old form.

He recognized that his history and community gave him an understanding of the world many people do not possess. With it, he created an ambiguous work expansive enough to affirm and celebrate many complexities of Black gay life. And from there, Riggs had no intention of stopping or slowing down. In fact, he was emboldened like never before: "Having come through that fire, they can't touch me."

A DISTINCTIVE CHARACTER

New challenges call for new forms. As the shapes of the issues we confront evolve, so too must our solutions. We need to allow our work to defy people's expectations and our own past practices, to find the forms that expand our thinking beyond the rigid conceptualizations we've grown accustomed to, and give us the freedom to articulate full-bodied pictures of success.

Reflecting on the brilliance of Black feminist readings of complex material and conditions, Chanel Craft Tanner said, "We don't search for the ambiguity, but we don't refuse it either." Our responsibility is to bring it in if that's what we need to do.

CONCLUSION

Did you win, he asked.
It wasn't a match, I say. It was a lesson.

— CLAUDIA RANKINE

In times of change, it helps to have somewhere to return. Lately, I've found myself revisiting a line from Yasunari Kawabata's short novel, *The Master of Go*. Ostensibly about a match between two players, the book by Japan's first Nobel Laureate is seen as an allegory for times of deep cultural shift. About two-thirds of the way in, Kawabata's narrator reflects on the way some insights are celebrated while others lie dormant.

"Examples must be legion," he says, "of wisdom and knowledge that shone forth in the past and faded towards the present, that have been obscured through all the ages and into the present but will shine forth in the future."

That such an orientation serves as a site of returning may be unsurprising at this point. After all, ambiguity is exactly the

CONCLUSION

type of timeless wisdom Kawabata speaks of. But what strikes me most is how eminently comfortable he appears to be with the ebb and flow of knowledge. Kawabata seems unbothered by the idea that a flawed narrative might dominate our lives for a period while what we truly need sits obscured. Like a thread on a loom that has dipped out of sight only to arise again in a new place, ambiguity sits ready, always, to be of use and shine forth again. *Don't worry*, Kawabata seems to say, *what we need will return.*

There is a comforting sense of faith in Kawabata, and he shares this with the figures profiled throughout the book. It isn't that they never wavered in the face of great odds, or even that they were sure everything would inevitably get better. Rather, they all possessed a faith in the worthwhile nature of the work before them. They believed that they had it within themselves to figure out what would work, that the wisdom and strength they needed to accomplish all they were after would be there when it was needed most.

Harriet Tubman faced incalculable odds and the ultimate danger in liberating people from slavery, both before and during the Civil War. In addition to a strong spiritual faith, she held an unshakeable faith not in the nation to do right, but in her own power to free others.

Cesar Chavez, Dolores Huerta, and Larry Itliong were up against a local political machine that included everyone from grape growers to the police. Guiding their years-long effort to win better pay and conditions for farm workers was a belief

AMBIGUITY IS THE ANSWER

that, despite all the work required to outmaneuver the other side, in the end, the practical victories and enduring legacy would make it all worthwhile.

Jane Jacobs and Mark Suster both knew what it meant to face off against an opponent who was much better resourced than they were. Their faith in the possibility of success, regardless of the odds, made it possible to overcome the inevitable attacks and feelings of futility, and keep going even when times were tough.

Thurgood Marshall was keenly aware of how the law codified and justified injustice, yet he also believed in its possibility for righting wrongs. On top of this, he had faith that future generations, like ours, would take up the fight for justice in their own ways and pass along a better society.

The legacy of the Tupac Amaru Rebellion has carried on long after the life of its namesake ended. As just one example, nearly two centuries later, Afeni Shakur named her son in honor of the Peruvian rebel. Tupac Amaru Shakur, better known as 2-Pac, went on to become one of the most influential and outspoken artists of all time. Reflecting the same faith that prompted the rebellion, he told an interviewer that while he might not be the one to change the world, "I guarantee that I will spark the brain that will change the world."

This faith is important because, as tempting as it is to try to tie our work directly to our impact, it isn't always possible. At a certain point, we must trust that the long arc of our lives

CONCLUSION

will carry on beyond us, that our legacies will stretch out in surprising and meaningful ways.

When I set out to write this book, I began with an inkling of ambiguity's strategic power. Over the course of researching and writing, my awe at ambiguity's capabilities has only grown. I'm more convinced than ever that we'll need to lean on ambiguity's usefulness in the years to come. The wisdom we need will return. My hope is we'll be prepared to put it to use.

There is no denying, however, that we are living in a heyday for rigidity and categorization. But these dominant ideologies are bumping up against their limits. They've become rote and restrictive. *Empty.* They're no longer convincing. No longer useful. We find ourselves believing in them less and less, and it's no mystery why: They aren't getting us anywhere better.

This brings us to the second trait beacons of ambiguity have in common. If we look closely, there is a resistance baked into all of them. They resist dumbing down who they are or carving themselves up into digestible parts. They resist being pressured into bad decisions and regressing to the mean. Time and again, in moments when everyone else would moderate—would *normalize*—beacons of ambiguity resist. They know exactly which way they are expected to go and choose not to go there.

In separate ways, Frantz Fanon and Virginia Woolf saw how dominant storylines sought to influence the way they and others saw themselves. Rather than accepting these as singular truths, they resisted them, choosing instead to view them in

AMBIGUITY IS THE ANSWER

tandem with knowledge held in the hidden transcripts, which they both believed had the potential to change the nature of people's lives.

Jim Burton knew what was expected of him to climb the ranks and fulfill his lifelong dream, but he resisted the moral compromises it would require of him. Instead, he lived out his principles and used ambiguity to outsmart an institution hellbent on sidelining him.

Marlon Riggs had achieved success and recognition using traditional forms of filmmaking but, in wanting to tackle a new set of experiences, he resisted the temptation to use standardized approaches. Instead, he expanded the shape of his work and created a film capable of accomplishing many things at once.

Perhaps the clearest example is Billie Holiday, who actively resisted easy description, choosing instead to proudly exist "beyond category."

In recent years, I have seen a deep yearning among people for new ways of working, seeing situations, and being themselves. It often feels like the options are narrowing at the same time that people need more. So if there is a secondary purpose to this book, it is to serve as an overdue antidote to the restrictive expectations placed on us. In maybe the simplest sense, *Ambiguity Is the Answer* is meant to serve as a reminder that it is okay to not do what is expected and to pursue new strategies instead. It is a reminder that we can move in new ways, embody more layers, and create with novel forms. We can resist the pressures

CONCLUSION

we face and maintain an unrelenting faith in the worthwhile nature of our work, just like the figures throughout this book.

As power concentrates against more of us, the world needs people who are comfortable exploring, embodying, and using ambiguity to create change. My hope is this book helps you feel a little more freedom, and makes you a little more able, to bring ambiguity into the important work you're doing. Because we need you. We really do.

NOTES

EPIGRAPH

"It is brave..." Gwendolyn Brooks, "do not be afraid of no," in *The Essential Gwendolyn Brooks*, ed. Elizabeth Alexander (New York: Library of America, 2005), 35.

INTRODUCTION

simple supposition A nod to the first line of Howard Zinn's essay "The Problem Is Civil Obedience" in *The Zinn Reader: Writings on Disobedience and Democracy* (New York: Seven Stories Press, 1997), 436.

A large body See: Jamie Holmes, *Nonsense: The Power of Not Knowing* (New York: Broadway Books, 2015); Daniel Kahneman, *Thinking, Fast and Slow* (New York: Farrar, Straus and Giroux, 2013).

MAKE IT. PROTECT IT. PASS IT ON.

"Our greatest responsibility..." Quoted in *Learning from the Future: Competitive Foresight Scenarios* (New York: John Wiley & Sons, 1998), eds. Liam Fahey and Robert M. Randall, 322.

contentious and drawn out The path to Marshall joining the Supreme Court is laid out most effectively in: Wil Haygood, *Showdown: Thurgood Marshall and the Supreme Court Nomination That Changed America* (New York: Knopf, 2015).

man walking Haygood, *Showdown*, 73.

Marshall was considered Haygood, *Showdown*, 62.

AMBIGUITY IS THE ANSWER

"His were the…" Haygood, *Showdown*, 344.

Marshall helped write Haygood, *Showdown*, 347-48.

A home he once Haygood, *Showdown*, 180-84.

meeting in London Juan Williams, *Thurgood Marshall: American Revolutionary* (New York: Three Rivers Press, 1998), 286.

intimate condescension Haygood, *Showdown*, 146-47.

series of papers The story about Einstein's papers is detailed in Walter Isaacson, *Einstein: His Life and Universe* (New York: Simon & Schuster, 2008), 90-106.

As the founder Haygood, *Showdown*, 62.

"He had a…" Quoted in Haygood, *Showdown*, 86.

abolitionist saying James Oakes, *The Scorpion Sting: Antislavery and the Coming of the Civil War* (New York: W. W. Norton, 2014).

"He was trying…" Quoted in Mashaun D. Simon, "'Moral Authority': How Justice Thurgood Marshall Transformed Society," *NBC News*, July 7, 2017, https://www.nbc news.com/news/nbcblk/moral-authority-justice-thurgood-marshall-transformed-so-ciety-n779821.

"The artist constantly…" Albert Camus, "Create Dangerously," in *Resistance, Rebellion, and Death* (New York: Vintage Books, 1995), 264.

future ancestor adrienne maree brown, *Emergent Strategy: Shaping Change, Changing Worlds* (Chico: AK Press, 2017), 14.

"delicate balance of turmoils" "The Tension of Change," *Time*, September 19, 1955. https://content.time.com/time/subscriber/article/0,33009,865192-1,00.html.

"like a map…" *United States Report Volume 510: Cases Adjudged in The Supreme Court, October Term 1993*, XX https://www.supremecourt.gov/opinions/boundvolumes/510bv. pdf.

In *Sweatt v. Painter* Haygood points to these four cases specifically in *Showdown*, 4-5. Case details for *Sweatt v. Painter*, *Smith v. Allwright*, *Shelley v. Kraemer*, and *Brown v. Board of Education* are discussed throughout both Haygood, *Showdown*, and Williams, *Thurgood Marshall*.

NOTES (PAGES 6-19)

Their widespread use See: Richard Rothstein, *The Color of Law: A Forgotten History of How Our Government Segregated America* (New York: Liveright, 2018); Keeanga-Ya-mahtta Taylor, *Race for Profit: How Banks and the Real Estate Industry Undermined Black Homeownership* (Chapel Hill: University of North Carolina, 2019).

"It shows how deep..." Quoted in Williams, *Thurgood Marshall*, 150.

unanimous decision Williams, *Thurgood Marshall*, 151.

"I was so happy..." Quoted in Williams, *Thurgood Marshall*, 226.

thirty-two cases Mark Tushnet, "Lawyer Thurgood Marshall," *Stanford Law Review* 44, Summer 1992, 1277, https://doi.org/10.2307/1229060.

nineteen as solicitor general Carl T. Rowan, *Dream Makers, Dream Breakers: The World of Justice Thurgood Marshall* (Boston: Little, Brown and Company, 1993), 295.

"Behind every one..." Howard Zinn, *The Politics of History* (Urbana: University of Illinois, 1990), 152.

invitation from Lincoln University This story comes from Isaacson, *Einstein*, 505.

"an American tradition..." Quoted in Isaacson, *Einstein*, 505.

"This is your democracy..." Thurgood Marshall, "Commencement Address, University of Virginia (May 21, 1978)," in *Thurgood Marshall: His Speeches, Writings, Arguments, Opinions, and Reminiscences*, ed. Mark V. Tushnet (Chicago: Lawrence Hill Books, 2001), 280.

almost forty years later Marianna Sotomayor, Phil McCausland, and Ariana Brock-ington, "Charlottesville White Nationalist Rally Violence Prompts State of Emer-gency," *NBC News*, August 12, 2017, https://www.nbcnews.com/news/us-news/torch-wielding-white-supremacists-march-university-virginia-n792021.

"must be considered..." Quoted in *Jet*, February 22, 1993, 5.

"He did what..." Quoted in Williams, *Thurgood Marshall*, 392.

TRUST IN THE LONG ARC

"One must wait..." Quoted in Robert Caro, *The Power Broker: Robert Moses and the Fall of New York* (New York: Vintage Books, 1975), 1.

AMBIGUITY IS THE ANSWER

"bright bedclothes" Gwendolyn Brooks, "when you have forgotten Sunday: the love story," in *The Essential Gwendolyn Brooks*, ed. Elizabeth Alexander (New York: Library of America, 2005), 7-8.

fifty thousand people Neil Steinberg, "50 Years Ago Chicago Squirmed at Picasso's 'Big, Homely, Metal Thing,'" *Chicago Sun-Times*, August 10, 2017.

Twelve hundred square feet Patricia Balton Stratton, *The Chicago Picasso: A Point of Departure* (Chicago: Ampersand, 2017), 10.

Four years earlier Stratton, *Chicago Picasso*, 25.

even more items Stratton, *Chicago Picasso*, 30.

Hartmann's firm Stratton, *Chicago Picasso*.

"a place waiting…" Richard M. Bennet, "Prose poem written to Picasso to urge the artist to design a sculpture for the City of Chicago," in Stratton, *Chicago Picasso*, 106.

On that Tuesday Stratton, *Chicago Picasso*, 8-10.

"Wings of justice" Quoted in Steinberg, "50 years."

knew **Chicago** See, for instance, Chapter 10 in: Angela Jackson, *A Surprised Queenhood in the New Black Sun: The Life & Legacy of Gwendolyn Brooks* (Boston: Beacon Press, 2017), 184-197. Also see: "A Conversation with Gwendolyn Brooks," in *Conversations with Gwendolyn Brooks* (Jackson: University Press of Mississippi, 2003), ed. Gloria Wade Gayles, 3, where Studs Terkel says to Gwendolyn Brooks "We think of you as Chicago."

"Does man like Art?" Gwendolyn Brooks, "The Chicago Picasso," in *The Essential Gwendolyn Brooks*, ed. Elizabeth Alexander (New York: Library of America, 2005), 91-92.

"with the belief…" Quoted in Stratton, *Chicago Picasso*, 68.

"I don't pick it up…" Iconoclasts, "Dave Chappelle and Maya Angelou," *Sundance Channel*, 46 minutes, November 30, 2006.

"We live in deeds…" Philip James Bailey, *Festus* (London: William Pickering, 1852), 49, https://www.google.com/books/edition/Festus/DD9aAAAAMAAJ?hl=en.

"They give us something..." This phrasing is inspired by Youngme Moon, *Different: Escaping the Competitive Herd* (New York: Crown Business, 2010).

NOTES (PAGES 19-32)

"calculated to baffle..." Quoted in Stratton, *Chicago Picasso*, 10.

"There are years…" Zora Neale Hurston, *Their Eyes Were Watching God* (New York: Harper, 2006), 21.

"Set…" Gwendolyn Brooks, "The Chicago Picasso, 1986, written for the 20th anniversary in 1987," in Stratton, *Chicago Picasso,* 105.

"a mind extender" "Gwendolyn Brooks Reading from Her Poetry," *Library of Congress*, September 30, 1985, https://www.loc.gov/item/85755182/.

CONFLICT COMES

"To learn which questions…" Ursula K. Le Guin, *The Left Hand of Darkness* (New York: Ace, 2019), 164.

Christopher Street This story has been told many times. See: Anthony Flint, *Wrestling with Moses: How Jane Jacobs Took On New York's Master Builder and Transformed the American City* (New York: Random House, 2009), 3-5. Also: Robert Kanigel, *Eyes on the Street: The Life of Jane Jacobs* (New York: Knopf, 2016), 68-69.

formed the foundation Jane Jacobs, *The Death and Life of Great American Cities* (New York: Vintage Books, 1992).

Fur District Kanigel, *Eyes*, 65-66.

"Each packet of furs…" Jane Butzner, "Where the Fur Flies," *Vogue*, November 15, 1935, 103, https://archive.vogue.com/article/1935/11/15/where-the-fur-flies.

During the 1920s See: James F. Wilson, *Bulldaggers, Pansies, and Chocolate Babies: Performance, Race, and Sexuality in the Harlem Renaissance* (Ann Arbor: University of Michigan, 2011); Angela Davis, *Blues Legacies and Black Feminism: Gertrude "Ma" Rainey, Bessie Smith, and Billie Holiday* (New York: Vintage Books, 1999); George Chauncey, *Gay New York: Gender, Urban Culture, and the Making of the Gay Male World 1890-1940* (New York: Basic Books, 1994).

the piers "Greenwich Village Waterfront: Christopher Street Pier, Manhattan," *NYC LGBT Historic Sites Project*, https://www.nyclgbtsites.org/site/greenwich-village-waterfront/.

"hope and lament..." Brittney Cooper, "On Hope and the Will to Fight," *The Remix*, June 1, 2022, https://theremix.substack.com/p/on-hope-and-the-will-to-fight.

AMBIGUITY IS THE ANSWER

Certain shifting dynamics For a discussion of these dynamics in current and historical geopolitics, see: Graham Allison, *Destined for War: Can America and China Escape Thucydides's Trap?* (New York: Houghton Mifflin Harcourt, 2017).

breeds conflict Roger V. Gould, *Collision of Wills: How Ambiguity about Social Rank Breeds Conflict* (Chicago: University of Chicago, 2003).

"a great power…" Quoted in Allison, *Destined for War*, 49.

Mark Suster has lived This story and quotes comes from Mark Suster, "The Surest Sign You're Winning Is When Goliath Takes a Swing at You," *Both Sides of the Table*, May 18, 2017, https://bothsidesofthetable.com/the-surest-sign-your-winning-is-when-goliath-takes-a-swing-at-you-da4103f80025.

trees of Birnam Wood William Shakespeare, "The Tragedy of Macbeth," in *The Norton Shakespeare: Tragedies* (New York: W. W. Norton & Company, 2008), eds. Stephen Greenblatt, Walter Cohen, Jean E. Howard, and Katharine Eisaman Maus.

a billion dollars Jeffrey Dastin and Greg Roumeliotis, "Amazon Buys Startup Ring in $1 Billion Deal to Run Your Home Security," *Reuters*, February 27, 2018, https://www.reuters.com/article/us-ring-m-a-amazon-com/amazon-buys-startup-ring-in-1-billion-deal-to-run-your-home-security-idUSKCN1GB2VG.

Having never graduated See: Flint, *Wrestling*.

"Nobody likes to practice…" Jacobs, *Death and Life*, 125.

"This book is an attack…" Jacobs, *Death and Life*, 3.

when Jacobs and her fellow organizers See: Flint, *Wrestling*.

infamous power broker See: Robert Caro, *The Power Broker: Robert Moses and the Fall of New York* (New York: Vintage, 1975).

"being nibbled to death by ducks" Kanigel, *Eyes*, 239.

WHEN THE METRICS DON'T MATCH

"The world changes…" Quoted in John Romano, "James Baldwin Writing and Talking," *New York Times*, September 23, 1979, https://www.nytimes.com/1979/09/23/archives/james-baldwin-writing-and-talking-baldwin-baldwin-authors-query.html.

NOTES (PAGES 32-55)

The day Charles Darwin This chapter relies heavily on Janet Browne, *Charles Darwin: The Power of Place* (New York: Alfred A. Knopf, 2003).

"I never saw a more striking..." Browne, *Charles Darwin*, 15.

Darwin praised Wallace Charles Darwin, *On the Origin of Species* (New York: Penguin, 2009), 12.

"survival of the fittest" Browne, *Charles Darwin*, 312.

"incommensurable" Thomas Kuhn, *The Structure of Scientific Revolutions* (Chicago: University of Chicago Press, 2012). 4.

"Neither problems nor puzzles..." Kuhn, *Structure*, 75.

"Although I am fully convinced..." Darwin, *Origin*, 420.

RETREAT AND RISE

"They will not know..." Sandra Cisneros, *The House on Mango Street* (New York: Vintage, 1991), 110.

no one understood this better See: Hayden Herrera, *Frida: A Biography of Frida Kahlo* (New York: Perennial, 2002).

"I want an absolutely..." Herrera, *Frida*, 88.

Galileo was instrumental David Wootton, *Galileo: Watcher of the Skies* (New Haven: Yale University Press, 2010).

set himself to studying See: Galileo Galilei, *Dialogues Concerning Two New Sciences* (Amherst: Prometheus, 1991); J. E. Gordon, *Structures: Or Why Things Don't Fall Down* (Cambridge: Da Capo Press, 2003), 27-28, 46, 89; Wootton, *Galileo*, 233-234.

On this particular day Plato, *Laches and Charmides* (Indianapolis: Hackett, 1992), trans. Rosamond Kent Sprague.

"Good heavens, Socrates..." Plato, *Laches and Charmides*, 31.

"the most important..." Iconoclasts, "Dave Chappelle and Maya Angelou," *Sundance Channel*, 46 minutes, November 30, 2006.

"to change your way...." Iconoclasts, "Chappelle and Angelou."

175

AMBIGUITY IS THE ANSWER

"who advances without…" Sun Tzu, *The Art of War* (Mineola: Dover, 2002), trans. Lionel Giles, 80.

"a step backward..." Kurt Vonnegut, *Player Piano* (New York: Dial, 2006), 312

powerful novel Ralph Ellison, *Invisible Man* (New York: Vintage International, 1995).

He moved to an illuminated For a photographic interpretation, see: *Invisible Man: Gordon Parks and Ralph Ellison in Harlem* (Göttingen: Steidl/The Gordon Parks Foundation/The Art Institute of Chicago, 2017), 105.

"A hibernation is a covert…" Ellison, *Invisible Man*, 13.

METABOLIZE MOMENTS

"I try not to find…" Maya Lin, *Boundaries* (New York: Simon & Schuster, 2000), 3:04.

September 8, 1965 Miriam Pawel, *The Crusades of Cesar Chavez: A Biography* (New York: Bloomsbury Press, 2014), 105-106. This chapter relies heavily on Pawel.

more than a thousand Eugene Nelson, *Huelga: The First Hundred Days of the Great Delano Grape Strike* (Delano: Farm Worker Press, 1969), 20-21.

$1.40 per hour Pawel, *Crusades*, 105.

1,200 Mexican American Mark Day, *Forty Acres: Cesar Chavez and the Farm Workers* (New York: Praeger: 1971), 39.

"Nobody knew exactly…" Dolores Huerta in ViewFinder, "Delano Manongs," *ALL ARTS*, 26:50, May 6, 2014, https://www.allarts.org/programs/viewfinder/kvie-viewfinder-delano-manongs/.

"to metabolize experience…" Audre Lorde, "Learning from the 60s," *Sister Outsider: Essays and Speeches* (New York: Ten Speed Press, 2010), 135.

"Instead of a rich definition…" Erving Goffman, *The Presentation of Self in Everyday Life* (New York: Anchor Books, 1959), 85.

a man named Lee Sedol This story comes from Cade Metz, "In Two Moves, AlphaGo and Lee Sedol Redefined the Future," *Wired*, March 16, 2016, https://www.wired.com /2016/03/two-moves-alphago-lee-sedol-redefined-future/.

"Lee Sedol needs to…" Quoted in Metz, "Two Moves."

NOTES (PAGES 55-73)

grower-friendly sheriff Pawel, *Crusades*, 113-114.

The growers sprayed Pawel, *Crusades*, 107.

Cessna airplane Pawel, *Crusades*, 108.

fifty farm workers Pawel, *Crusades*, 124-130.

after five years See: Pawel, *Crusades*.

REMEMBER THE POWER OF SECRETS

"If ever you are tempted..." Quote slightly edited from Epictetus, "Enchiridion," in *Discourses and Selected Writings* (New York: Penguin, 2008) trans. Robert Dobbin, 229.

Harriet Tubman never divulged Catherine Clinton, *Harriet Tubman: The Road to Freedom* (New York: Back Bay Books, 2004), 37.

"When I found..." Quoted in Kate Clifford Larson, *Bound for the Promised Land: Harriet Tubman, Portrait of an American Hero* (New York: One World, 2003), 84.

false promises of freedom See, for instance, Clinton, *Harriet Tubman*, 14, 29.

"the function of freedom..." Toni Morrison, "Cinderella's Stepsisters," in *The Source of Self-Regard: Selected Essays, Speeches, and Meditations* (New York: Vintage, 2020), 111.

everything reinforced Edward E. Baptist, *The Half Has Never Been Told: Slavery and the Making of American Capitalism* (New York: Basic Books, 2016).

In 1850 See: Clinton, *Harriet Tubman*, 53, 60. Also: Andrew Delbanco, *The War Before the War: Fugitive Slaves and the Struggle for America's Soul from the Revolution to the Civil War* (New York: Penguin Press, 2018); Eric Foner, *Gateway to Freedom: The Hidden History of the Underground Railroad* (New York: W. W. Norton & Company, 2016); James Oakes, *Freedom National: The Destruction of Slavery in the United States, 1861-1865* (New York: W. W. Norton & Company, 2014).

aligned with the seasons Clinton, *Harriet Tubman*, 85-86.

They helped how and where See: Foner, *Gateway*. Also: William Still, *The Underground Railroad: Authentic Narratives and First-Hand Accounts* (Mineola: Dover, 2007), ed. Ian Frederick Finseth.

"found it impossible..." Foner, *Gateway*, 152.

177

AMBIGUITY IS THE ANSWER

"Is there no way…" Quoted in Foner, *Gateway*, 215

"the wide terrain…" Stephanie M. Camp, *Closer to Freedom: Enslaved Women and Everyday Resistance in the Plantation South* (Chapel Hill: University of North Carolina Press, 2004), 2.

funerals Clinton, *Harriet Tubman*, 47.

reveal Robert Caro, *The Passage of Power* (New York: Knopf, 2012), xiv.

"camouflage is less necessary" Caro, *Passage*, xiv.

to Union lines Oakes, *Freedom National*.

June 2, 1863 Clinton, *Harriet Tubman*, 165-167. For a comical version of the Combahee River Raid, see: Drunk History, "Harriet Tubman Leads an Army of Bad Bitches (ft. Octavia Spencer)," *Comedy Central*, 5:33, https://www.youtube.com/watch?v=VpTf1GFjCd8.

official Confederate report Clinton, *Harriet Tubman*, 168.

Had it not been Oakes, *Freedom National*, 381.

"the applause of the crowd" Frederick Douglas, "Letter from Frederick Douglass," in Sarah Hopkins Bradford, *Harriet: The Moses of Her People: A Biography of Harriet Tubman* (Public Domain: originally published in 1886), 81.

LOVE YOUR LAYERS

"How to explain…" Maggie Nelson, *The Argonauts* (Minneapolis: Graywolf Press, 2015), 53.

A wiry man The story of Pham Xuan An and Nguyen Thi Ba meeting up in the market is from Larry Berman, *Perfect Spy: The Incredible Double Life of Pham Xuan An* (New York: Smithsonian, 2007), 42-49. For more on An and Ba's relationship, see: Hoàng Hải Vân and Tấn Tú, *Phạm Xuân Ẩn: A General of the Secret Service* (Hà Nội: Giớ, 2008), 125-132.

"truly one of the oddest..." Berman, *Perfect Spy*, 46.

The journalist's name See: Robert Sam Anson, *War News: A Young Reporter in Indochina* (New York: Touchstone, 1989).

NOTES (PAGES 73-90)

An was a cornerstone For Pham Xuan An biographical information, see: Berman, *Perfect Spy*; Thomas A. Bass, *The Spy Who Loved Us: The Vietnam War and Pham Xuan An's Dangerous Game* (New York: Public Affairs, 2009).

Viet Thanh Nguyen was thinking Viet Thanh Nguyen, Zoë Ruiz, Lisa Sanchez Powers, Cathy McGregor Weingeist, Brian McGovney, Bogdan Suceavă, Lance Heard, Gerald Sato, and Tom Lutz, "Book Club Redux: 'The Sympathizer,'" *Los Angeles Review of Books*, March 3, 2107 https://lareviewofbooks.org/article/book-club-redux-the-sympathizer/.

"the best kind of truth" Viet Thanh Nguyen, *The Sympathizer* (New York: Grove, 2015), 121.

"The truth?" Quoted in Morley Safer, *Flashbacks: On Returning to Vietnam* (New York: St. Martin's, 1991), 280-281.

"keeping alive" Trinh T. Minh-ha, "Film as Translation: A Net with No Fisherman," in *Framer Framed* (London: Routledge, 1992), 116.

"I can only say…" Quoted in Berman, *Perfect Spy*, 226.

special thanks David Halberstam, *The Making of a Quagmire* (New York: Random House, 1965), Author's Note.

"It is a story…" Quoted in Bass, *Spy*, 4.

feelings were representative Berman, *Perfect Spy*, 248-263.

One friend of An's Bass, *Spy*, 234.

"he is a reminder…" Quoted in Berman, *Perfect Spy*, 5.

"So it was…" Nguyen Khai, *Past Continuous* (Willimantic: Curbstone, 2001), trans. Phan Thanh Hao and Wayne Karlin, 136.

trip back to Vietnam Anson, *War News*, 309-313

NOISE IN THE SILENCE

"And there are those…" Khalil Gibran, *The Prophet* (Ballingslöv: Wisehouse, 2015), 30.

banned from professional boxing Dave Zirin, "June 20, 1967: Muhammad Ali Convicted for Refusing the Vietnam Draft," *Zinn Education Project*, https://www.zinnedproject.org/news/tdih/-muhammad-ali-convicted-refusing-vietnam-draft.

AMBIGUITY IS THE ANSWER

George Foreman Dave Anderson, "Ali Regains Title, Flooring Foreman," *New York Times*, October 30, 1974, https://archive.nytimes.com/www.nytimes.com/learning/general/onthisday/big/1030.html.

one billion "Oct 30, 1974 CE: Rumble in the Jungle," *National Geographic*, https://education.nationalgeographic.org/resource/rumble-jungle/.

Both boxers began *Muhammad Ali: When We Were Kings: The Untold Story of the Rumble in the Jungle*, directed by Leon Gast (1996; Universal City, CA: Universal Studios, 2005), DVD.

"Get off the ropes, Ali!" ESPN, *Ali vs Foreman*, ESPN+, https://www.espn.com/espnplus/player/_/id/2037e461-9726-455a-92f4-1fe206d64d02.

"That all you got, George?" Don Burke, "Muhammad Ali Dead at 74," *New York Post*, June 4, 2016, https://nypost.com/2016/06/04/muhammad-ali-dead-at-74/.

"I realized that this ain't..." Burke, "Muhammad Ali."

"The thing they said..." ESPN, *Ali vs Foreman*.

"Power is not only…" Saul Alinsky, *Rules for Radicals: A Pragmatic Primer for Realistic Radicals* (New York: Vintage Books, 1989), 127.

"wide terrain" Stephanie M. Camp, *Closer to Freedom: Enslaved Women and Everyday Resistance in the Plantation South* (Chapel Hill: University of North Carolina Press, 2004), 2.

"strategic performances of ambiguity…" Ralina L. Joseph, *Postracial Resistance: Black Women, Media, and the Uses of Strategic Ambiguity* (New York: New York University Press, 2018), 29.

nominated for five Television Academy, "Abbott Elementary: Awards & Nominations," *Emmys*, https://www.emmys.com/shows/abbott-elementary.

Ralph was so stunned Television Academy, "Supporting Actress in a Comedy Series: 74th Emmy Awards," *YouTube*, https://www.youtube.com/watch?v=cRw8IFLS1Fs.

rather than congratulating Television Academy, "Writing for a Comedy Series: 74th Emmy Awards," *YouTube*, https://www.youtube.com/watch?v=zRgs1mexjrU.

NOTES (PAGES 90-101)

"strategy of reading simultaneity" Valerie Smith, *not just race, not just gender: Black Feminist Readings* (New York: Routledge, 1998), xv.

outlets like Newsweek Jamie Burton, "Jimmy Kimmel Accused of Stealing Quinta Brunson's Spotlight with Emmy Joke," *Newsweek*, September 13, 2022, https://www.newsweek.com/jimmy-kimmel-accused-quinta-brunson-emmys-joke-1742425.

and USA Today Suzette Hackney, "Jimmy Kimmel's Stupid Antics Are Just Latest Insult for Black Women (and Men) in Hollywood," *USA Today*, September 13, 2022, https://www.usatoday.com/story/opinion/columnist/2022/09/13/quinta-brunson-jimmy-kimmel-emmys/10366695002/?gnt-cfr=1.

Sheryl Lee Ralph made it clear Selome Hailu, "Sheryl Lee Ralph Addresses Jimmy Kimmel Crashing Quinta Brunson's Emmys Speech: 'Ooh, the Disrespect!'" *Variety*, September 14, 2022, https://variety.com/2022/tv/news/sheryl-lee-ralph-jimmy-kimmel-quinta-brunson-emmys-1235372648/.

Brunson made an appearance Jimmy Kimmel Live, "Quinta Brunson & Jimmy Kimmel on Emmys Controversy," *Youtube*, September 14, 2022, https://www.youtube.com/watch?v=00qB_d7i3ZA.

"wink at certain audiences..." Joseph, *Postracial Resistance*, 29.

KEEP MOVING

"The most effortful…" Daniel Kahneman, *Thinking, Fast and Slow* (New York: Farrar, Straus and Giroux, 2013), 37.

given an ultimatum The story of Jim Burton and the Bradley Fighting Vehicle is told in James G. Burton, *The Pentagon Wars: Reformers Challenge the Old Guard* (Annapolis: Naval Institute Press, 1993).

"dump" Quoted in Myra MacPherson, "The Man Who Made War on a Weapon," *Washington Post*, May 8, 1986, https://www.washingtonpost.com/archive/lifestyle/1986/05/08/the-man-who-made-war-on-a-weapon/7b47ff0e-59df-4201-845c-d19b1597b395/.

"rolling death trap" Quoted from William Boly, "The Army's $11-Billion Deathtrap," *Reader's Digest*, August 1983, condensed from *California Magazine*, February 1983, in Burton, *Pentagon Wars*, 136.

AMBIGUITY IS THE ANSWER

"culture of procurement" James Fallows, *National Defense* (New York: Random House, 1981), 62.

"there's nothing to do…" Paul Beatty, *The Sellout* (New York: Picador, 2015).

"symbiotic ties…" Walter Isaacson, "The Winds of Reform," *Time*, March 7, 1983, 26, https://time.com/vault/issue/1983-03-07/page/1/.

"Jim, you may not win…" Burton, *Pentagon Wars*, 67.

Boyd's landmark revelation Robert Coram, *Boyd: The Fighter Pilot Who Changed the Art of War* (New York: Back Bay, 2002), 327-339.

when Steve Kerr took over Baxter Holmes, "The Charcuterie Board That Revolutionized Basketball," *ESPN*, October 11, 2017, https://www.espn.com/espn/feature/story/_/page/enterpriseWarriors/how-steve-kerr-revolutionized-golden-state-warriors-offense-charcuterie-board.

"The main goal…" Quoted in Holmes, "Charcuterie."

the team averaged Analysis from "NBA Advanced Stats," *NBA*, Regular Season: 2014-2015, 2015-2016, 2016-2017, 2017-2018, 2018-2019, 2019-2020, 2020-2021, 2021-2022, https://www.nba.com/stats/teams/passing.

The mistake The explanation of how momentum and ambiguity work together, as well as the elements people so often get wrong, comes from Coram, *Boyd*.

what better testing ground This phrasing is an adaptation of a point made by Coram, *Boyd*, 402.

"little brothers and sisters" Quoted in Coram, *Boyd*, 138.

"If something needs to leak..." Quoted in Coram, *Boyd*, 405.

"strategies must be pursued…" Frances Fox Piven and Richard A. Cloward, *Poor People's Movements: Why They Succeed, How They Fail* (New York: Vintage Books, 1979), 37.

public frustration See: Fallows, *National Defense*.

"When they surprise you…" Coram, *Boyd*, 403.

"I'll get back with you" Burton, *Pentagon Wars*, 180.

"Ambiguity" Coram, *Boyd*, 338.

NOTES (PAGES 101-126)

HARNESS HIDDEN TRANSCRIPTS

"Our favorite people..." Joan Didion, *Slouching Towards Bethlehem* (New York: Farrar, Straus and Giroux, 2008), 71.

In lectures to crowds Virginia Woolf, *A Room of One's Own* (Orlando: Harcourt, 2005).

"the accumulation of..." Woolf, *Room*, 88.

"hidden transcripts" James C. Scott, *Domination and the Arts of Resistance: Hidden Transcripts* (New Haven: Yale University, 1990), x.

"a peculiar visceral intelligence" Homi Bhabha, "Foreword: Framing Fanon," in Frantz Fanon, *The Wretched of the Earth* (New York: Grove, 2004) trans. Richard Philcox, ix.

"serve not only as inhibitors..." Fanon, *Wretched*, 16

Fanon spent much of his life Frantz Fanon, *The Wretched of the Earth* (New York: Grove, 2004) trans. Richard Philcox.

"definitions belonged to..." Toni Morrison, *Beloved* (New York: Vintage, 2004), 225.

NEVER UNDERESTIMATE FLUIDITY

"All greatness is improbable" Lao Tzu, "Three Treasures," in *Tao Te Ching: A Book about the Way and the Power of the Way* (Boulder: Shambhala, 2019), version by Ursula K. Le Guin, 80.

ships out of steel See: J. E. Gordon, *Structures: Or Why Things Don't Fall Down* (Cambridge: Da Capo, 2003), 64-65.

By the 1990s See: Naomi Oreskes and Erik M. Conway, *Merchants of Doubt: How a Handful of Scientists Obscured the Truth on Issues from Tobacco Smoke to Global Warming* (New York: Bloomsbury, 2011), 169-215.

"The industry had realized..." Oreskes and Conway, *Merchants*, 18.

"One Last Shower of Petals" "One Last Shower of Petals," in *Japanese Tales* (New York: Pantheon, 1987), ed. and trans. Royall Tyler.

"Gold, Gold" Lieh Tzu, "Gold, Gold," in *Chinese Fairy Tales and Fantasies* (New York: Pantheon, 1979) ed. and trans. Moss Roberts with C. N. Tay.

AMBIGUITY IS THE ANSWER

Aesop's fables *Aesop's Fables* (Watermill Press, 1985).

One of Nelson Mandela's favorite "The Enchanting Song of the Magical Bird" trans. Darrel Bristow-Bovey, in *Favorite African Folktales* (New York: W. W. Norton, 2004), ed. Nelson Mandela.

In the 1770s See: Charles F. Walker, *The Tupac Amaru Rebellion* (Cambridge: Belknap Press, 2014).

"Spanish America..." Quoted in Walker, *Tupac*, Epigraph.

"powered the engine..." Ward Stavig, *The World of Tupac Amaru: Conflict, Community, and Identity in Colonial Peru* (Lincoln: University of Nebraska, 1999), xviii.

"The Spanish had initially..." Walker, *Tupac*, 35.

"He had the respect..." Walker, *Tupac*, 5.

"With structures..." Gordon, *Structures*, 63.

THE APPEAL OF NOT KNOWING

"If you can't be free..." Rita Dove, "Canary," in *Collected Poems: 1974-2004* (New York: W. W. Norton, 2017), 213.

Though Harlem Somini Sengupta, "Where Jazz Put Its Feet Up; Many Black Musicians Made Their Homes in Queens," *New York Times*, September 20, 1998, https://www.nytimes.com/1998/09/20/nyregion/where-jazz-put-its-feet-up-many-black-musicians-made-their-homes-in-queens.html.

On Saturday afternoons John Szwed, *Billie Holiday: The Musician and the Myth* (New York: Penguin, 2015), 44.

Holiday was This chapter relies heavily on Farah Jasmine Griffin, *If You Can't Be Free, Be a Mystery: In Search of Billie Holiday* (New York: Free Press, 2001).

bisexual Black woman Griffin, *If You Can't*, 30, 53-54.

new notions of freedom Angela Davis, *Blues Legacies and Black Feminism: Gertrude "Ma" Rainey, Bessie Smith, and Billie Holiday* (New York: Vintage Books, 1999).

"amplified moments..." Saidiya Hartman, *Wayward Lives, Beautiful Experiments:*

NOTES (PAGES 126-137)

Intimate Histories of Riotous Black Girls, Troublesome Women, and Queer Radicals (New York: W. W. Norton, 2019), xiv-xv.

"I don't know what it is…" Billie Holiday with William Dufty, *Lady Sings the Blues* (New York: Harlem Moon, 2006), 43.

"beyond category" John Edward Hasse, *Beyond Category: The Life and Genius of Duke Ellington* (New York: Da Capo, 1993).

"This, I always figured…" Holiday with Dufty, *Lady*, 43.

rooted in the blues See, for instance: LeRoi Jones (Amiri Baraka), *Blues People: Negro Music in White America* (New York: William Morrow, 1999). As Farah Jasmine Griffin and Robert G. O'Meally have pointed out, *Blues People* holds historical pairing with Ralph Ellison's review of the book: Ralph Ellison, "Blues People," in *Living with Music: Ralph Ellison's Jazz Writings* (New York: Modern Library, 2002), ed. Robert G. O'Meally. See: Griffin, *If You Can't*, 124-125.

"the blues is an art of ambiguity" Ellison, *Living with Music*, 48.

a song about longing See, for example, Robert O'Meally, *Lady Day: The Many Faces of Billie Holiday* (Boston: Da Capo, 1991), 165. Also: Davis, *Blues Legacies*.

"dual possibility" Fred Moten, *In the Break: The Aesthetics of the Black Radical Tradition* (Minneapolis: University of Minneapolis Press, 2003), 10.

"She was able to set…" Davis, *Blues Legacies*, 180.

"often baffles when it most intrigues" Ellison, *Living with Music*, 98.

"It's probably going to be a mess" Quoted in "Huffington Post," *Tig Notaro*, http://tignation.com/web/huffington-post/.

Hello, good evening. Tig Notaro, *Live* (Bloomington: Secretly Canadian, 2013), Digital.

Barely more than a week Tig Notaro, *I'm Just a Person* (New York: Ecco, 2016), 129.

"It's going to be okay" Notaro, *Live*.

surpassed 100,000 copies Madeline Raynor, "Tig Notaro Will Tour and Perform in the Homes of Her Fans in Her New Showtime Special," *IndieWire*, July 2, 2013, https://www.indiewire.com/features/general/tig-notaro-will-tour-and-perform-in-the-homes-of-her-fans-in-her-new-showtime-special-37149/.

AMBIGUITY IS THE ANSWER

"It's a startling release…" Stuart Heritage, "Tig Notaro and Her Jaw-Dropping Cancer Routine." *The Guardian*, October 12, 2012, https://www.theguardian.com/culture/2012/oct/19/tig-notaro-reveals-cancer-on-stage.

"an amazing, uncomfortable document" Gavin Edwards, "Louis C.K. Selling Tig Notaro's Instantly Legendary Comedy Set," *Rolling Stone*, October 5, 2012, https://www.rollingstone.com/tv-movies/tv-movie-news/louis-c-k-selling-tig-notaros-instanly-legendary-comedy-set-204609/.

"I can't really describe it" "Huffington Post," *Tig*.

"something I don't think…" HuffPost Video, "How Tig Notaro Brought Louis CK to Tears," *HuffPost*, https://www.huffpost.com/entry/how-tig-notaro-brought-louis-ck-to-tears_n_5b564939e4b07de723e96b8c.

"The more we claim…" Griffin, *If You Can't*, 65.

"never goes where we expect…" Griffin, *If You Can't*, 89.

In early 1959 Griffin, *If You Can't*, 114-115.

INTRODUCE ALTERNATIVES

"Everything you see…" Yasiin Bey (fka Mos Def), "Thieves in the Night," *Mos Def and Talib Kweli Are Black Star* (New York: Rawkus, 1998), CD.

"Forced into certain circumstances…" Anne Truitt, *Daybook: The Journal of an Artist* (New York: Scribner, 2013), 140.

ability to endure Truitt, *Daybook*, 35.

"It can be, quite literally…" Truitt, *Daybook*, 35.

"A familiar brunt" Truitt, *Daybook*, 35.

"it occurred to me…" Truitt, *Daybook,* 35.

birds in the *Anthoscopus* genus Guy M. Kirwan, Steve Madge, Joseph del Hoyo, Nigel Collar, and Peter F. D. Boesman, "African Penduline-Tit (*Anthoscopus caroli*)," *Birds of the World*, ed. Brooke Keeney (Ithaca: Cornell Lab of Ornithology), September 24, 2021, https://doi.org/10.2173/bow.afptit1.02.

NOTES (PAGES 138-151)

Kobe Bryant was 30 for 30, "Sole Man," *ESPN Films*, 77:24, April 16, 2015, https://www.espn.com/espnplus/catalog/e9280267-4643-4a53-87e3-aca7321d10f5/sole-man.

"Most players..." Quoted in Larry Brown, "How Kobe Bryant Manipulated His Way to Lakers on Draft Day," *Fox Sports*, June 25, 2015, https://www.foxsports.com/stories/nba/how-kobe-bryant-manipulated-his-way-to-lakers-on-draft-day.

twenty seasons "Kobe Bryant Stats," *ESPN*, https://www.espn.com/nba/player/stats/_/id/110/kobe-bryant.

81 in a single game NBA.com Staff, "Top Moments: Kobe Bryant Drops 81 Points on Raptors in 2006," *NBA*, September 14, 2021, https://www.nba.com/news/history-top-moments-kobe-bryant-81-points-2006.

won five NBA championships NBA.com Staff, "Kobe Bryant: A Basketball Legend," *NBA*, February 25, 2020, https://www.nba.com/kobe-bryant-tribute.

major invasion See: Anthony Cave Brown, *Bodyguard of Lies* (New York: Harper & Row, 1975).

"the first of a series" Quoted in Brown, *Bodyguard*, 675.

A DISTINCTIVE CHARACTER

"All I want to know..." Formatted into sentence form from the poem Essex Hemphill, "For My Own Protection," in *In the Life: A Black Gay Anthology* (Washington: Redbone Press, 2008), ed. Joseph Beam, 174.

pictured his friend Gene Marlon Riggs, "Letter to the Dead," *Breakthrough*, Spring 1993, 17-21, http://www.freedomarchives.org/Documents/Finder/DOC501_scans/Break/501.break.24.spr.93.pdf.

groundbreaking film *Tongues Untied*, DVD, directed by Marlon Riggs, in *The Signifyin' Works of Marlon Riggs* (New York: The Criterion Collection, 2021).

"standing upright..." Riggs, "Letter," 18.

wasn't necessarily expected Robert Anbian, "Tongues Untied Lets Loose Angry, Loving Words: An Interview with Marlon Riggs," *Release Print*, March 1990, 5-6, 15-18, https://newsreel.org/guides/Riggs-Guide/Release-Print-Riggs-Interview-1990.pdf.

"Riggs's unclassifiable scrapbook..." Wesley Morris, "Blackness, Gayness, Represen-

AMBIGUITY IS THE ANSWER

tation: Marlon Riggs Unpacks It All in His Films," *New York Times*, February 6, 2019, https://www.nytimes.com/2019/02/06/arts/blackness-gayness-representation-marlon-riggs-unpacks-it-all-in-his-films.html.

like a journalist Public Affairs, "Berkeley Talks Transcript: Late Filmmaker Marlon Riggs on Making 'Tongues Untied,'" *Berkeley News*, January 15, 2021, https://news.berkeley.edu/2021/01/15/berkeley-talks-transcript-marlon-riggs-bampfa-1990/.

"I had to say the things…" Quoted in Public Affairs, "Berkeley."

"My feeling is that…" Quoted in Ron Simmons, "Tongues Untied: An Interview with Marlon Riggs," in *Brother to Brother: New Writings by Gay Black Men* (Washington: Redbone Press, 2007), ed. Essex Hemphill, 237.

premiered in San Francisco This story and quotes are from Riggs, "Letter."

"My life is of value and..." Quoted in Simmons, "Tongues," 237.

"If the world were…" Quoted in Israel Shenker, "E. B. White: Notes and Comments by Author," *New York Times*, July 11, 1969, https://archive.nytimes.com/www.nytimes.com/books/97/08/03/lifetimes/white-notes.html.

on June 5, 1981 Randy Shilts, *And the Band Played On: Politics, People and the AIDS Epidemic* (New York: St. Martin's Press, 1987), 68-69.

Five young gay men "Pneumocystis Pneumonia—Los Angeles," *Morbidity and Mortality Weekly Report* 30, no. 21: 1-3, https://www.cdc.gov/mmwr/preview/mmwrhtml/june_5.htm.

Cleve Jones remembered Cleve Jones, *When We Rise: My Life in the Movement* (New York: Hachette, 2016), 195.

"By 1985…" Jones, *When We Rise*, 204.

"That's how we lived then" Jones, *When We Rise*, 232.

one of dysfunction See: Shilts, *Band*; Sarah Schulman, *Let the Record Show: A Political History of ACT UP New York, 1987-1993* (New York: Farrar, Straus and Giroux, 2021).

"Once all susceptible members…" "Why Make AIDS Worse Than It Is," *New York Times*, June 29, 1989, https://www.nytimes.com/1989/06/29/opinion/why-make-aids-worse-than-it-is.html.

NOTES (PAGES 151-167)

"What AIDS revealed…" Quoted in Schulman, *Let the Record Show*, 372.

"distinctive character" Steven Epstein, *Impure Science: AIDS, Activism, and the Politics of Knowledge* (Berkeley: University of California Press, 1996), 10.

It took on a form For an overview of the range of activities in New York City, as one example, see Schulman, *Let the Record Show*.

simultaneity of action Schulman, *Let the Record Show*, 28.

"It was a simultaneous approach…" Schulman, *Let the Record Show*, 471.

It was during the filming Karen Everett, *I Shall Not Be Removed: The Life of Marlon Riggs*, 1996, DVD.

"Funny how crisis has a way…" Riggs, "Letter," 19.

In order for *Tongues Untied* Julia Lesage and Chuck Kleinhans, "Interview with Marlon Riggs: Listening to the Heartbeat," *Jump Cut*, no. 36, 1991, 119-126,   https:// webapps.cspace.berkeley.edu/cinefiles/imageserver/blobs/0b4728e5-d974-43a2-8dce/ content/linked_pdf.

The film won awards Simmons, "Tongues Untied," 239.

"Having come through that fire…" Quoted in "Tongues Untied," *Frameline,* https:// www.frameline.org/distribution/films/tongues-untied.

"We don't search for the ambiguity…" Chanel Craft Tanner, "Fucking with the Grays," *The Remix*, May 19, 2022, https://theremix.substack.com/p/fucking-with-the-grays.

CONCLUSION

"Did you win?…" Claudia Rankine, *Citizen: An American Lyric* (Minneapolis: Graywolf Press, 2014), 159.

"Examples must be legion…" Yasunari Kawabata, *The Master of Go* (New York: Vintage International, 1996), 120.

ACKNOWLEDGMENTS

Spending the time to work on this book has been rewarding in ways far beyond what I ever imagined. I feel blessed to have been able to work on such a meaningful project and hope everyone will have the chance to be engaged so deeply in a project of their choosing.

As has been the case for so many writers before me, I did much of my work for this book in the margins of the day. Before the kids woke up. Riding on busses and trains. While dinner cooked. And because it is made up of life as much as research, I am overtaken by a fear of leaving out the names of anyone who not only shared feedback and guidance over the years but also, simply, time together. So to all the friends and family who've been there for me at any point over the years, thank you, thank you, thank you. Please accept my blanket love and appreciation and know that it includes you. I hope you're not only proud of what I've done here, but of the person I've been along the way. May the future hold even more moments for us to be together.

I feel enormous gratitude for those whose lives and work

went into these pages. Thank you for sharing your brilliance with the world. I can't count the number of times you've left me in awe. It has been an absolute privilege to spend so much time with you and your ideas.

My sincere appreciation to those friends and family who took the time to read early versions and share your thoughts. Having such thoughtful and caring folks to turn to is an honor in itself. Your insights undoubtedly strengthened the work, and I value your contributions immensely.

My involvement with the Kelly Strayhorn Theater has been especially meaningful while writing this book. Thank you to the community, staff, and board, past and present, for continually building the organization into such a beautiful home for so many of us. I'm deeply appreciative of the time we've spent together, and so hopeful for what the future holds.

As much as I've loved all the researching and writing that went into this book, in looking back, it's clear to me that my favorite moments were the interruptions. Words can't express how much I've loved putting down the laptop in the morning to cuddle on the couch with Nora, or watching Imogen dance on top of the manuscript while a record plays. The book was only made better by these moments.

None of this would have been possible without the love, support, and perspective of my incredible wife, Jess. Thank you for believing in me, and for building a life with me that is more beautiful and hilarious than I knew was possible.

And thank you, for reading.

A NOTE ON THE TYPE

The wreath of roses icon used on the first page of each chapter is from VTC Harriet, a font designed by Tré Seals at Vocal Type and named in honor of Harriet Tubman. The font characters depict quilt designs believed to have been used by the Underground Railroad to secretly convey messages to those escaping to freedom. The wreath of roses design serves as a remembrance for all those who lost their lives seeking liberation.

All other text in this book is set in Carol Twombly's modern take on the Caslon font from the 17th century. One of a small number of women leading the design of new fonts at the onset of digital typefaces, Twombly's work built on a long tradition of women's under-recognized labor and design choices in crafting new letter forms. She designed some of the most popular fonts in the world, including letters etched in stone at the Maryland State House monument to Thurgood Marshall, then left the corporate world to create art.

INVITATION

If the stories and ideas in here have resonated with you in some way, I truly hope you'll take me up on my invitation for you to contact me and connect.

You can reach me directly at the email below:

kyle@fallowpress.com